TWILIGHT
AND
PHILOSOPHY

The Blackwell Philosophy and Pop Culture Series

Series Editor: William Irwin

TWILIGHT
AND
PHILOSOPHY

VAMPIRES, VEGETARIANS,
AND THE PURSUIT OF
IMMORTALITY

Edited by
Rebecca Housel and
J. Jeremy Wisnewski

WILEY

John Wiley & Sons, Inc.

To Twilight *fans of all ages, both living and undead.*

CONTENTS

ACKNOWLEDGMENTS

Supernatural Humans We Can't Live Without

Jeremy and Rebecca would like to collectively thank the contributors of this book for their extraordinary efforts, the team at Wiley who made this project come to life, including Connie Santisteban and Lisa Burstiner, and of course the series editor, William Irwin, for his incredible editorial instincts as well as his pop culture and philosophical prowess—are you sure you're not a Cullen?

Jeremy thanks his posse for their willingness to put up with endless nonsense and equally endless obsession. Thanks, Dorothy and Audrey. (He'd also like to thank his new son, Lucian Xavier Wisnewski, just because he wants the boy to be thanked in a book—it's an auspicious start.) Jeremy also wants to thank Meg Lonergan for her patience with proofreading and her toleration of quirks. She's been a great help over the past couple of years.

Rebecca conveys hearty appreciation to Laura Smith-Savoca and Jenny Geissler for prepurchasing *Twilight* tickets, getting to the theater early, and patiently waiting in line with all the tweens and teens so Rebecca could see the movie opening day—what an experience! She also thanks Stephenie Meyer for creating the *Twilight* universe, Stephen King for being a literary inspiration, and J. K. Rowling for helping to expand the possibilities of the middle-grade/young-adult genre. Abigail Myers gets a shout-out along with Derek Harrison, Ethan Schwartz, Jaime Freedman, and Marguerite Schwartz. Thanks to Mary Conley-Thomas and Eva Schwartz-Barson for being inspirational women who instill a love of story in all their grandchildren and great-grandchildren, and last but certainly not least, Gary, Bob, and Bell for *all* you do!

INTRODUCTION
Undead Wisdom

Freud once claimed that love and death mark the driving forces of human existence. Having fallen in love with the undead of *Twilight*, we might well say the same thing about this vampire tale. The *Twilight* books confront love and death, and so much more, in a way that facilitates a strange recognition—that the dead are indeed wise, and that they are sometimes wise in matters of the heart, even when that heart doesn't beat. The strange beauty of *Twilight* lies here, as elsewhere: we are all faced with death, and we all desire to love. These two facts—one deeply unpleasant, the other quite pleasant—are evident in *Twilight*. This makes for great reading, and as you will soon see, it also provides great philosophical opportunities.

Death is everywhere. It is between any two syllables, waiting to choke the final breath out of you. It is a force like no other: inescapable, ineffable, and absolute—at least for mere mortals. Death captivates. It haunts. The thought that somehow death might not master us enchants the mind until we find ourselves drawn again and again to the hope that we might escape our fate—by being made immortal vampires, or finding an afterlife, or through a scientific "cure" for death. There is little as powerful as the thought of death, and probably little that motivates us in the way that our mortality does.

Except perhaps love. The existentialist philosopher Albert Camus (1913–1960) once claimed that the only real philosophical question was whether or not to kill yourself in the face of an absurd world. The writer Tom Robbins thinks one can only answer this question with one even more basic: Are you able to love? For love, Robbins suggests, is the only thing that makes life worth living. Love allows us to see things we could never see without it. It shapes our perceptions of the world and enables us to be open to deep, meaningful experiences. It can change a humdrum little town in Washington into a world of wonder.

In the world of *Twilight*, death is not inevitable, and the purest form of love seems to have been found. Such a world not only allows an exploration of the human condition— facing our deepest and darkest fears, as well as our highest hopes. It also *demands* that we explore our condition—and there is no better companion for such an exploration than philosophy.

The *Twilight* saga is full of love and death, as well as a host of other topics central to the way we understand ourselves and navigate the world. Philosophical issues permeate the pages of the *Twilight* books. Bella and Edward are a mirror for our greatest fears and hopes—for all that can go right with our lives and all that can go wrong. They are the human condition writ large, there for our reflection and exploration.

Perhaps surprisingly, we have a lot to learn from the undead, as well as from the way they relate to the living— about ourselves, our experiences, and our relationships with other people. This book aims to help you with just that, asking such questions as: What is the nature of love? Is death something to be feared? How should feminists react to Bella

Swan? Is there a moral obligation to be vegetarian? What is it like to experience the world as a vampire? What does it mean to be a person? How free are we?

Forks, Washington, is a small town; unfortunately, minds can be very small places, too. But philosophy has a way of opening up both: It allows us to see what we hadn't seen before and allows us to explore issues we might not otherwise explore. Only literature rivals philosophy in this capacity, making our examination of the *Twilight* saga the perfect place for literature and philosophy to meet.

So whether you're a fan of Edward Cullen or Jacob Black, believe Bella a fool or a romantic, or are a vegan or a carnivore, keep reading! You'll enjoy chapters on everything from why we love vampires to how Edward is a Byronic hero to the Tao of Jacob, and much more.

PART ONE

TWILIGHT

one

YOU LOOK GOOD ENOUGH TO EAT: LOVE, MADNESS, AND THE FOOD ANALOGY

George A. Dunn

There is always a bit of madness in loving. But there is also always a bit of reason in madness.

—Friedrich Nietzsche[1]

Edward Cullen is doomed. The new girl sitting next to him in biology class looks and—to make matters even worse—*smells* good enough to eat. In fact, in the century or so he's been stalking the Earth, Edward has never before inhaled a fragrance quite so intoxicating. His nostrils have in their delirium taken the rest of his brain hostage. His sanity is on its way to becoming a dim memory, along with all that gentlemanly self-restraint he's worked so long and hard to cultivate.

All he can think about is what he'd like to do with this girl once he gets her alone—and how he can make that happen. Blinded and blindsided by this sudden upsurge of appetite, he's able to regain control of himself just long enough to bolt out the door and drive to Alaska, where a couple of days of cool mountain air does the work of a long, cold shower, sobering him up and chilling him out.

Philosophy requires a fearless dedication to the truth, so let's be completely honest with each other right here at the outset: Who among us can't relate to this experience? Not that your designs on that scrumptious cupcake seated next to you in biology class (or whatever class it was) were *exactly* the same as Edward's. Heaven forbid! But there's not a soul among us who doesn't have at least some appreciation of what this poor guy is going through. Who hasn't been ambushed by a desire that strikes with such abrupt force that it becomes nearly impossible to hide its presence, let alone to resist being yanked in whatever direction it wants us to go? Protest all you like, but I think you know exactly what I'm talking about. But if you insist on denying that you've ever been slapped silly by a sudden rush of desire, then the kindest thing I can say is that you're probably not a very promising candidate for the study of philosophy—at least not according to the ancient Greek philosopher Plato (428–348 BCE), whom we shall be meeting shortly.

"Sorry about the Food Analogy"—What's Your Pleasure?

On first glance, Edward's experience seems to be something entirely unique to members of his species, since it's the smell of Bella Swan's blood that arouses him and there's nothing figurative about his desire to consume her. "Sorry about the food analogy," he says to Bella when, in his clumsy attempt to explain his boorish behavior toward her on the day they meet, he ends up comparing her to ice cream.[2] Of course, for most of us this really would be no more than an analogy. The delectable eye candy sitting next to you in class wasn't *really* a cupcake, and you probably didn't *literally* want to take a bite out of the apple of your eye. But there's something a bit disingenuous about Edward calling *his* food reference an "analogy," since he really did want to make a meal of Bella.

Edward's experience isn't entirely strange to us, because erotic and romantic longings really do seem to share something in common with physical hunger. And who can doubt that this food analogy—the way that a vampire feeding on his victim can serve as a metaphor for an amorous conquest—accounts for a considerable part of the eroticism of vampire fiction? What else could it be? There's nothing inherently sexy about being hundreds of years old (or even Edward's more tender age of only one hundred and eighteen) and always maintaining the temperature of a corpse. But there is something undeniably erotic and intimate about the way a vampire feeds, not to mention the seductive animal magnetism he exudes, through which he effortlessly charms his victims into surrendering their wills and baring their throats. Of course, in the *Twilight* saga, it's Bella who's incessantly trying to wear down Edward's rock-ribbed resistance. But the Cullen boy is a peculiarly honorable bloodsucker.

In any case, it can't be an accident that the language of food offers such a rich and felicitous store of metaphors for describing our experience in the seemingly very different domain of sex and romance. No doubt this fact is in part because eating is one of life's most intensely sensual pleasures. We delight in the appearance, aroma, and taste of our food. Our muscles engage in the agreeably sensuous activities of biting, chewing, and swallowing each tasty morsel. Once we've reduced our food to a pulp and pushed it down the esophagus, our contented stomach repays us for the boon via brain boost, radiating a feeling of profound satisfaction to the rest of the body. Each step of the process brings its own distinctive form of pleasure, so it's with good reason that eating, along with drinking, is closely associated with being merry. For newborns, both human and vampire, the sensual pleasure of feeding offers us our earliest experience of gratification, securing a place for eating as one of our principle paradigms of deep carnal joy. And by a happy coincidence, eating is also the principal activity through which the joyful pulse of life's vitality is sustained. We eat in obedience to the commands of nature, and nature rewards our obedience by making eating a genuine pleasure. Our sexual appetite is like this, too—nature's need is our delight. In both hunger and erotic desire, the force of biology finds a powerful ally in the lure of pleasure.

Of course, the analogy isn't perfect. The activity of eating ends up destroying the object of our enjoyment—or at least putting an end to its existence as an independently existing entity by transforming it into part of our own flesh. Lovers, on the other hand, never literally become one flesh, however tightly they cling to each other. Nonetheless, the world is full of predatory amorists who exploit others in much the same way the rest of us gobble down our meals, showing as little regard for the welfare of their partners as the lion shows for the lamb.

But even if we follow the chivalrous example of Edward— the lion who fell in love with the lamb—and recognize that our beloved has needs and interests of her own that set a limit to how far we can go in indulging our desires, it remains true that every form of sensual enjoyment resembles somewhat the pleasures of eating.[3] Enjoyment is always a matter of "imbibing" or being "filled" with sensations that are essentially private or solitary in nature, even when the source of enjoyment is a shared activity like lovemaking. Moreover, we can get so swept up in a flood of pleasure that nothing beyond our present enjoyment seems to matter. Even gentlemanly Edward has to admit that his craving for Bella's company is essentially selfish, motivated by a desire to feast on her beauty and fragrance, a voluptuous banquet for the sake of which he's willing to put his beloved at mortal risk.[4]

"What I Knew Was *Right* . . . and What I *Wanted*"

The cover of the first book of the *Twilight* saga depicts outstretched hands cupping a bright red apple, bringing to mind another famous connection between the alimentary and the amorous that's deeply embedded in Western consciousness. Most of us are familiar with the story of the Fall of Humanity found in Genesis, the first book of the Bible, which narrates how the first man and woman lost their original childlike innocence and were expelled from paradise as a result of disobeying God's command not to eat the fruit of "the tree of the knowledge of good and evil" (Genesis 2:17). The Bible, of course, never explicitly identifies the "forbidden fruit" as an apple. But perhaps because apples figured so prominently in Greek mythology as catalysts of desire and discord, someone must have assumed that an apple also was the most likely culprit in the Genesis story, and the idea stuck.[5] The Bible also never directly implicates lust as a factor in the Fall. But that didn't deter many early Christian theologians from insisting that the "knowledge of good and evil" imparted by the forbidden fruit had something to do with *carnal knowledge*, an interpretation supported by Adam and Eve's sudden discovery of their nakedness upon partaking of the fruit.[6] Consequently, forbidden desire has been associated ever since with taking a big juicy bite out of an apple.

When medieval Christian theologians such as Thomas Aquinas (1224–1274) contemplated that apple, they believed it was alerting us to the dangers of what they called *concupiscentia*, or "concupiscence." That was their word for the perfectly

natural and spontaneous movement of desire toward pleasurable things, like food and sex. Of course, there's nothing
inherently bad about these objects of desire. In fact, Aquinas
insisted they were necessary and good, but—and this is a crucial qualification—only as long as we seek them not solely for
pleasure but rather for the sake of the purposes for which he
believed God intended them, such as nourishing our bodies
and reproducing the species. Allowed to operate outside the
constraints of conscience and reason, concupiscent desires
become tinder for sins like lust and gluttony. Aquinas clas-
sified concupiscence as a form of love, but distinguished it
from friendly affection in that the object of concupiscence
"is loved, not that any good may come to it, but that it may
be possessed."[7] Our desire to eat is concupiscent since we are
interested in only the nutrients and enjoyment we can take for
ourselves. Erotic desires are concupiscent too, since they aim
at our own pleasure.

Concupiscent desires are powerful, pleasurable, and—in
the opinion of Aquinas and other Christian moralists—nothing but trouble when they come to dominate the personality.
Not only do they incline us toward immoderate and harmful
forms of self-indulgence, but when we start to view other people exclusively through the distorting lens of concupiscence,
we end up reducing them to mere objects to be consumed or
enjoyed. And that's pretty much how we're viewed by most
vampires outside the Cullen clan. "Happy Meals on legs" is
the description of human beings favored by Spike from *Buffy
the Vampire Slayer*—another vampire partial to food analo-
gies.[8] For a frightening picture of how Aquinas might have
imagined pure, unbridled "concupiscence on legs," we need
only consider the newborn vampires depicted in *Eclipse*. They
are, as Edward puts it, "[b]loodthirsty, wild, out of control."[9]
If these frenzied, amoral appetites run amok are what desire
tends to become when left unsupervised by our better rational nature, then let's man those embattled ramparts of reason.

Edward found himself teetering atop those ramparts one night in Bella's bedroom. Earlier that day he had discovered he had a potential rival in Mike Newton, and the resultant feelings of jealousy inflamed his desire for Bella to the point that breaking and entering seemed a reasonably good idea. That night he made his first of what were to become his nightly forays into Bella's bedroom to spy on his beloved while she slept. He later explained to Bella what was going through his head that first night: "I wrestled all night, while watching you sleep, with the chasm between what I knew was *right*, moral, ethical, and what I *wanted*. I knew that if I continued to ignore you as I should, or if I left for a few years, till you were gone, that someday you would say yes to Mike, or someone like him."[10]

We all know that it isn't Mike Newton—or even someone very much like him—who would have claimed Bella's heart if Edward hadn't come along. But however mistaken Edward may have been about his competition, his wrenching internal struggle was very real. Aquinas undoubtedly would have described it as a battle between concupiscence ("what I *wanted*") and conscience ("what I knew was *right*"). The tremendous power of concupiscence is demonstrated by the fact that hearing his name muttered by Bella in her sleep was all it took to persuade him to chuck conscience aside and go for the apple.

The Vampire Socrates

After all this talk about wanton appetites inducing us to do things that are stupid and wrong, we're ready at last to make the acquaintance of Plato, one of the greatest philosophers of all time, to ponder the problem of desire. One of the big recurring themes of Plato's philosophy was the phenomenon the Greeks knew as *erôs*, a word with a meaning that overlaps to some extent with the Latin *concupiscentia* but carries an even stronger connotation of irrationality. *Erôs* is the Greek word for passionate desire, typically, but not necessarily, sexual in nature and frequently associated with madness. For example, when the ancient Greek historian Thucydides (460–395 BCE) described the lust for the overseas empire that gripped the citizens of Athens when they set their sights on conquering the island of Sicily, he referred to it as their erôs, suggesting that this excessive passion crippled their judgment and led directly to their disastrous defeat at the hands of the Spartans in the Peloponnesian war.[11]

We might compare the Athenian's foolhardy expedition to another—and particularly foul—expression of erôs that we encounter in the *Twilight* saga: James's single-minded obsession with tracking and killing Bella, which also tempts him to engage in reckless behavior through which he courts his own ruin. Most often, erôs referred to the passion of being in love or to intense carnal lust. But as we learn from the examples of Edward, Bella, Jacob Black, Leah Clearwater, and other frequently unhappy residents of Forks and La Push, even the seemingly more benign forms of erôs can addle the mind and wreak havoc on the emotions.

No wonder, then, that some Greek thinkers regarded erôs as a menace. With the premium that philosophers place on reason and the reputation of erôs as a force of irrationality, we might expect the philosopher Plato to be among those cautioning us not to let erôs gain so much as a toehold in our souls. But *au contraire*! Plato, while never denying that erôs could be a form of madness, held the surprising view that madness wasn't necessarily a bad thing, even claiming that "the greatest of all good things come to us through madness, provided the madness is divinely given."[12] These are words that Plato attributed to Socrates (470–399 BCE), a fellow philosopher whom many believed exhibited more than a slight touch of madness himself and whom Plato featured as the principle interlocutor (or conversation partner) in all but a handful of the nearly three dozen philosophical dialogues that have been credited to him. In several of these dialogues—notably, the *Phaedrus* and the *Symposium*—passionate love is a chief topic of conversation, although erôs turns up as a subsidiary theme in many other places in the Platonic corpus, reflecting Plato's conviction that any experience this overwhelming and universal must reveal something fundamental about the human condition.

Plato seems to have picked up his interest in erôs from Socrates, whom he quoted in one dialogue as claiming "to know nothing except *the things of love*"—in Greek, *ta erôtica*.[13] Most books on ancient philosophy will tell you that Socrates was Plato's teacher or mentor, but in fact their relationship seems to have been based on something much deeper, more mysterious, and perhaps even more *erotic* than that. It would be much closer to the truth to call Socrates *il suo cantante*, Plato's singer, in the very same sense intended by the Volturi when they describe Bella to Edward as *la tua cantante*.[14] For Socrates' words sang to Plato—and not Plato alone—in the same enthralling accents as Bella's blood sings to Edward. Not that Plato and Socrates were sleeping with each other. There's no evidence that Socrates slept with *any* of the young men who swarmed around him to listen to his philosophical discussions, however much some of them may have desired that. In this respect, he appears to have been as chaste as Edward before taking his nuptial vows. As for Socrates' young admirers, many of them must have felt just like Bella, awakened from the stupor of their humdrum existence by an encounter with a dazzlingly charismatic figure who seemed to many of them downright *otherworldly*.

One of these admirers was the handsome and roguish Alcibiades (450–404 BCE) who, despite being the most prominent and desirable man in all of Athens, was thoroughly besotted with love for Socrates. Plato described how poor Alcibiades felt so bewitched by Socrates that he accused him to his face of being like the flute-playing satyr Marsyas, a mythical creature whose music was said to leave his listeners spellbound. "You differ from him only in this," Alcibiades told Socrates, "that you accomplish the same thing by bare words without instruments."[15] But the comparison is apt for more than just the way the impression made by Socrates' words resembled the effect of the satyr's legendary flute playing. Everyone agreed that Socrates' appearance was remarkably, even alarmingly, satyr-like—which is to say he was an ugly old cuss! With his short stature, corpulent midsection, thick neck, bulging eyes, snub nose, and bald head, it's unlikely that even vampire venom could have done much for his looks. But however ugly Socrates may have been on the outside, his devoted followers were filled with erôs for what they believed was his incomparably beautiful soul.

Although lacking the outer beauty and grace of vampires like the Cullens, Socrates still seemed like a bloodsucker to many. Even the nineteenth-century philosopher Søren Kierkegaard (1813–1855), who heard that old satyr's flute calling across the centuries, wrote that Socrates was to his young admirers like a "vampire who has sucked the blood of the lover and while doing so has fanned him cool, lulled him to sleep, and tormented him with troubling dreams."[16] But whether Socrates was an *evil* vampire depends on whom you ask. The families of some of his followers—his victims, if you prefer—watched with alarm as members of Socrates' clique expressed their scorn for things such as honor, money, and political power—indeed for anything other than the pursuit of philosophical wisdom that Socrates advocated as the only thing worthwhile. But that's just what erôs does to a person. Everything that isn't associated with the beloved fades into insignificance. Just as Bella, after all that time spent in the company of immortals, couldn't help but regard her school prom as "some trite human thing" despite what it meant to her human friends, so the lovers of Socrates tended to lose their taste for the things of the mundane world from which they believed Socrates had rescued them.[17]

In the minds of most respectable Athenians, the strange spell that the "vampire" Socrates cast on his followers provided ample confirmation that erôs is madness. But at the same time, it persuaded Plato that Socrates was right to claim that some forms of madness can be divine.

Lambs and the Predators Who Adore Them

Plato composed a dialogue titled the *Phaedrus*, named after the young man of that name whom Socrates engaged one day in a long conversation on the topic of erôs. Phaedrus has just read Socrates a speech written by the famous orator Lysias (445–380 BCE), who describes falling in love as a terrible sickness that enfeebles the judgment and causes those it afflicts to behave in a shameful manner. The lover is needy, controlling, easily wounded, unrealistic in his appraisal of his beloved's merits, and prone to resentment when the affair ends. We might add that some lovers will even enter your house uninvited, spy on you while you sleep, read the minds of your friends, hold you prisoner, and drag you to the prom against your wishes. Headaches and complications are the best you can expect from a relationship with someone who loves you, according to Lysias. Consequently, he concludes that "[sexual] favors should be granted to one who is *not* in love with you rather than to one who is."[18] Take a more rational approach to hanky-panky and minimize the emotional risks by pairing off with a "sex buddy" instead of some dangerous madman who has fallen in love with you.

Phaedrus is bowled over by Lysias's speech, but Socrates thinks it's terrible—not just because of its morally dubious conclusion but also because he thinks it's so poorly written and argued. After some goading by Phaedrus, Socrates reluctantly agrees to demonstrate how one could make a better argument—more clear, concise, and logical—on the same topic, composing his own rival speech denouncing love right there on the spot. His begins in a way that will sound familiar to us, distinguishing two contending forces that dwell within every human being, each of which would like to run the show.

> One of them is our inborn desire for pleasure, the other an acquired opinion in pursuit of the best. Sometimes the two, lodged within us, agree; at other times they quarrel. Then sometimes one, sometimes the other gains the upper hand. When right opinion with reason rules and leads toward the best, we call this moderation. But when desire irrationally drags us toward pleasure and rules over us, we call this excess.[19]

Irrational desire for the pleasures of food is gluttony, irrational desire for wine is drunkenness, and irrational desire for some fetching beauty is erotic love. And just like the glutton and the drunk, the lover approaches the object of his desire as something to be consumed and enjoyed, heedless of how he may be harming the one he is using for his pleasure. Does that ring a bell? How about this? The lover is crazy about his beloved, Socrates concludes, in exactly the same way that "wolves adore lambs."[20]

We've heard it all before—concupiscence and conscience, predators and prey, the *food analogy*. Poor maligned erôs! Doesn't anyone have anything *nice* to say about wild infatuation and smoldering passion? It turns out that Socrates does, after all.

Abruptly breaking off his speech in horror at his offense against the gods—he's defamed erôs, one of their greatest gifts—he launches into a new speech. Recanting his blasphemies, he now offers a hymn in praise of erôs, lauding it as a "divine madness" through which the souls of lovers sprout wings that can carry them to the greatest heights, even to heaven, the abode of the gods. His speech in praise of erôs is a tour de force, recognized today as a classic in the literature of love for both its memorable metaphors and the serious philosophical ideas they impart. His basic insight seems to be that when we love *rightly*—more in a moment on what that means—some mortal being can become a window through which higher dimensions of reality shine forth. When we see some lovesick fool doting on some clumsy, weak, imperfect creature, lavishing on her (or him) adoration that only a god could deserve, we may think we're witnessing an act of insanity. What we don't realize is that this lover may be glimpsing something higher than meets our sensible and sober eyes, something that really *is* unconditionally lovable.

"Other Hungers . . . That Are Foreign to Me"

None of this sounds very scientific. But Socrates could respond that love is just one of those bewildering experiences that may in the end be impenetrable to scientific reason. That doesn't imply we can't say anything intelligent and meaningful about it, though. Where sterile argument and analysis fail, as perhaps they must when we're dealing with something as unreasonable as love, Socrates resorts to mythmaking.

He thus invites us to imagine the soul as a chariot, driven by a charioteer and pulled by a team of two winged horses, one compliant and well-behaved, the other stubborn and unruly. Once upon a time, before we acquired our physical bodies, our souls dwelt in heaven, where they "banqueted upon" and were "nourished by"—there's that food analogy again—the unspeakably marvelous sight of absolute moral and spiritual perfection, the likes of which are glimpsed only in a dim and shadowy way here on Earth.[21] Here below in the physical realm we encounter many things that seem to be striving for perfection but never quite reach it. For example, *justice* is a virtue only imperfectly realized in some of our institutions, *moderation* something we are able to exercise only occasionally and imperfectly, and *knowledge* something we possess in only the most fallible and imperfect fashion.

Yet we must have some idea of perfection in order to be able to recognize these myriad forms of imperfection. Socrates' myth suggests that our idea of perfection is a dim memory of our heavenly existence, when we both gazed and feasted on the ideal forms of *justice, moderation, knowledge*, and other divine realities that have only defective likenesses on earth. We would be feasting on those visions of perfection today if not for a series of grievous mishaps and blunders that caused us to lose our wings and fall to Earth, where we're now imprisoned in needy and cumbersome bodies, forced to rely on defective senses that distract us from our memory of the grandeur we once beheld.

Socrates explains that in an imperfect world like ours, there's little that could serve as a reminder of the brilliant spectacle of those perfect beings that once nourished our souls. Even with the acute senses of a vampire, we still wouldn't be able to discern many traces of perfection here in this lower realm, where for the most part only imperfect things are visible. As Socrates observes, "There is no shine in the images here on earth of justice and moderation and the other things honorable for souls."[22] Lacking the splendor of their perfect heavenly counterparts, the imperfect instance of *justice* and *moderation* we encounter here on Earth doesn't have the power to reawaken memories of the deep satisfaction and joy we experienced in heaven. And so that joy is forgotten—unless and until we fall in love. For there's one form of perfection that shines in a way that even our feeble mortal senses can't easily miss: *beauty*, especially the beauty that shines from some dazzling creature whose presence alone is enough to flood the soul with erotic and romantic longings.

In heaven the sight of unalloyed *beauty*, contemplated in its pure electrifying radiance, was "the most blest of the mysteries" we beheld.[23] But even after we fell to Earth, "we grasped it shining most clearly through the clearest of our senses, because sight is the sharpest of our physical senses."[24] Socrates probably should have qualified that last statement, for while sight may be the sharpest sense for us mortal human beings, the sense of smell is the most acute for vampires. No surprise, then, that Edward's powerful longings were awakened by a *whiff*, rather than the more common *vision*, of perfection. But regardless of whether it's a beautiful form or a beautiful fragrance, *beauty* possesses a unique ability to remind us of a joy that lies beyond this world and therefore beyond mere carnal satisfactions.

But because the soul is complex remember those two horses, one compliant, the other unruly—our reaction to the sight (or *smell*, in Edward's case) of earthly beauty can be a tortured knot of conflicting emotions. On the one hand, the well-behaved horse is constrained by its sense of decency from pouncing straight away on that beautiful creature that looks (or smells) like a little piece of heaven. But the unruly horse feels no such restraint. It goes berserk and lurches forward, dragging the other horse and the charioteer along with it, all the while forcing them "to recall the delights of sex." Only when they "see the darling's face, flashing like a lightning bolt," refreshing the memory of "beauty itself standing alongside moderation on a holy pedestal," do the more orderly parts of the soul find the strength to restrain the rampaging lust of the unruly horse.[25] As Socrates describes it, the battle between the unruly horse and the other parts of the soul can be protracted and ugly, but if it ends with that misbehaving beast subdued, "the lover's soul follows the darling with awe and a sense of shame."[26]

This strange myth unfolds one of the fundamental mysteries of love, how reverence for one's beloved as a token of otherworldly perfection can cohabit with the most flagrantly carnal desires. To love rightly, on this account, is simply to get that unruly horse of carnal desire under control so that it doesn't rob of us love's most precious gift, the opening of a porthole through which fleeting glimpses of transcendent beauty can be spied. Edward knows this tension within the soul firsthand. "I wish you could feel the . . . complexity . . . the confusion . . . I feel," he stammers to Bella.[27] "I've told you, on the one hand, the hunger—the thirst—that, deplorable creature that I am, I feel for you. And I think you can understand that, to an extent . . . But . . . there are other hungers. Hungers I don't understand, that are foreign to me."[28]

Carnal lust is a desire to feast our senses on the voluptuous pleasures promised by the beloved's beautiful flesh, form, and in some cases fragrance. We know exactly what it would mean to sate that sort of desire. But Edward's experience of other, more mysterious "hungers" points to another, more mysterious feast and to satisfactions that reach us through channels other than the senses. Socrates' myth gives us a language for describing those satisfactions—feasting at a heavenly banquet on the pure forms of moral and spiritual perfection—but it's a poetic and metaphoric language that dispels none of the mystery of the experience of love.

"A Moonless Night"

But there's another aspect of Socrates' myth that we must not overlook. That boiling cauldron of lust that Socrates depicts as an unruly horse is the very thing that rouses the soul to approach the beloved in the first place! Without that troublemaking scalawag called concupiscent desire, no one would ever draw close enough to mortal beauty to detect within it intimations of something higher. Consequently, our lives would be like Edward's before he got his first whiff of Bella— sane, sober, and steady. Our lives would be "like a moonless night" with little "points of light and reason" but never a meteor flashing across the sky, dazzling us out of our listless complacency, and awakening strange longings.[29]

Traditional moralists may have a point when they urge us to be wary of our carnal appetites, especially if our appetites turn out to be anything like Edward's. But Socrates' myth suggests that we should be grateful for them as well. No doubt Edward is relieved that he could muster enough self-control to resist that "deplorable" hunger that nearly trampled his good sense and morals into the dirt that fateful day in biology class. But, having defeated the beast that wanted to consume Bella there on the spot, he's probably still very glad that it was there in the beginning to call his attention to the girl who smelled good enough to eat.

NOTES

1. *Thus Spoke Zarathustra: A Book for Everyone and Nobody*, trans. by Graham Parkes (New York: Oxford University Press, 2005), p. 36.

2. Stephenie Meyer, *Twilight* (New York: Little, Brown and Company, 2005), p. 267.

3. Ibid., p. 274.

4. Ibid., p. 266.

5. For example, when Paris of Troy judged a beauty contest among three goddesses, Aphrodite, Hera and Athena, he declared Aphrodite the winner and awarded her a golden apple. The other goddesses were such sore losers that they incited the Trojan War and brought about the destruction of Troy. Consider also the role of apples in the myths of Atalanta and the Garden of the Hesperides.

6. See Elaine Pagels, *Adam and Eve and the Serpent: Sex and Politics in Early Christianity* (New York: Vintage Books, 1989), pp. 27–28.

7. *The Summa Theologica of St. Thomas Aquinas, Volume One*, trans. by the Fathers of the English Dominican Province (Paris: Christian Classics, 1981), p. 299 (Pt. 1, Q. 60, Art. 3).

8. *Buffy the Vampire Slayer*, "Becoming (Part 2)," episode 222.

9. Stephenie Meyer, *Eclipse* (New York: Little, Brown and Company, 2007), p. 26.

10. *Twilight*, p. 303.

11. See *The Landmark Thucydides: A Comprehensive Guide to the Peloponnesian War*, ed. by Robert B. Strassler and trans. by Richard Crawley (New York: Touchstone Books, 1998), p. 373 (6.24.3).

12. *Plato's Phaedrus*, trans. by Stephen Scully (Newburyport, MA: Focus Philosophical Library, 2003), 24 (2444a).

13. *The Dialogues of Plato, Volume Two: The Symposium*, trans. by R. E. Allen (New Haven, CT: Yale University Press, 1993), p. 117 (177d) (emphasis added).

14. See Stephenie Meyer, *New Moon* (New York: Little, Brown and Company, 2006), p. 490.

15. *Dialogues of Plato*, 161–162 (215c–d, 216c).

16. *The Concept of Irony/Schelling Lecture Notes: Kierkegaard's Writings, Volume Two*, trans. by Howard V. Hong and Edna H. Hong (Princeton, NJ: Princeton University Press, 1992), p. 49.

17. *Twilight*, p. 496.

18. *Plato's Phaedrus*, 2 (227c).

19. Ibid., 16 (237d–238a).

20. Ibid., 20 (241d).

21. Ibid., 28 (247d–e).

22. Ibid., 31 (250b).

23. Ibid., 31 (250b–c).

24. Ibid., (250d).

25. Ibid., 35–36 (254a–b).

26. Ibid., 36 (254e).

27. *Twilight*, p. 277.

28. Ibid., pp. 277–278.

29. *New Moon*, p. 515.

DYING TO EAT: THE VEGETARIAN ETHICS OF *TWILIGHT*

Jean Kazez

Edward Cullen is the kind of vampire you'd want your daughter to date, if she had to date a vampire. It's particularly reassuring the way he's in control of his appetites. Bella Swan looks delicious to him, in every sense, but he knows what is allowed and not allowed (particularly in fiction suitable for teens). As ravenous as he is for humans, he abstains. You've gotta eat, though, and a vampire needs to feed on blood. Edward satisfies his nutritional requirements by feasting on animal blood, which makes him, he says, a vegetarian—by vampire standards. Animal blood is like tofu, for the Cullen family, but they live on a human-free diet anyway, because it's the right thing to do.

It's possible the Cullens subscribe to mainstream Western ideas about the status of animals—the idea that humans are in an exalted moral category, and the idea that animals exist to serve human purposes (or some such). But the movie version of *Twilight* also puts Edward's vampire vegetarianism in an interesting light, since it makes Bella a vegetarian too—the regular kind. Possibly the hamburger would be better, but she orders the mushroom ravioli or veggie burger when she goes out to eat.

Since Edward and Bella are kindred spirits, it's natural to think that their restrained diets have a similar ethical source. Edward's choice to eat animals, but not humans, does not then come from traditional disdain for animals; Bella's choice to eat mushroom ravioli, but not animals, isn't just a health decision. There's some ethical principle that both Bella and Edward would agree to, which leads in different directions in their different circumstances. But what is it?

A novel can't tell you everything about characters' lives, covering every bathroom break and trip to the drugstore. So I propose that one of the things left out of the *Twilight* books and the movie is that Edward and Bella took a night class at a college nestled in the pines on the outskirts of Forks. The class was called "The Ethics of Eating," and I speculate the happy couple fit right in with all of the other pale, grungy students, if Edward was just a shade paler. In this class, they endeavored to articulate what the common principle is that leads to their diverging ways of practicing the ethic of vegetarianism.

Scene 1. In Which a Reasonable Ethic Is Proposed

Edward and Bella must have insisted that ending the life of any animal, of any species, is a serious matter. You can't kill lightly, or for just any trivial reason, but a sufficiently serious reason can give you justification. The difference, then, between Bella's and Edward's diet stems from their reasons. Bella may like "food with a face" but has no serious reason to consume it, so she doesn't; but Edward does have a reason to kill—he can't survive without a blood meal—so he does.

Of course (they must have admitted), Edward has a serious reason to consume any animal food, human *or* nonhuman. He especially likes the taste of human blood. But taste is not enough. Since nonhuman blood will fulfill his requirements equally well, that's what he has to choose. If he must kill, it's better to kill a nonhuman animal.

The idea that it's better to kill a nonhuman animal may seem to be a reversion to standard Western animal dismissal, but that isn't really so. Without putting humans on a pedestal, we can recognize differences of value. Even Peter Singer, a leading ethicist and champion of animals, is willing to admit that typical members of different species have lives with different values.[1] If you are in the classic situation of the firefighter trying to decide whose life to save, a human or a dog, he says you ought to save the human before the dog, assuming both are typical members of their species. If the choice is between the dog and a goldfish, I think he'd have you save the dog.

If that makes sense, it doesn't follow that we're entitled to an across-the-board preference for human interests over animal interests, or dog interests over goldfish interests. Humans don't come first in every conceivable case. To think so would have to involve the bias in favor of humans that Singer calls "speciesism." But it's reasonable to ask yourself which loss is the more grave, if some life must be lost. Singer uses a homely analogy: if you dump a bottle of Kahlua down the drain, more is lost than if you dump a bottle of soy milk. What is lost when an animal dies depends on what "filled that bottle" to begin with.

On what basis do we make these value discriminations? It's a matter of dispute, but one approach is to consider what different species (or their typical members) are capable of.[2] Comparative psychologists and ethologists are discovering that there are no black-and-white distinctions. It's not empirically supportable to say that humans are rational and animals are entirely instinctive; in fact, humans are partly instinctive and animals partly rational. There's no empirical support for saying that humans have language and animals none at all. It's really not true that animals have *no* sense of self or *nothing* at all akin to morality.

What's true is that in each of these categories, humans do have more extensive and nuanced abilities. Of course, there are things animals are better at, too. Some birds migrate pole to pole, and others cache vast numbers of seeds in the winter, succeeding in finding most of them after they've been buried by snow in the winter. Cheetahs run at speeds above seventy miles per hour, making the best human athlete look impaired by comparison.

Still, if we do everything in our power to recognize and appreciate animal abilities, it's impossible to overcome the sense that there's "better stuff in our bottles." By all means, nonhuman lives have value and they "count," morally speaking, but you'd be saving the more precious life if you pulled a human being out of a fire before a dog or a mouse.

So much for our priorities in situations that involve saving lives. But the ethics of food raises questions about killing, not saving. The issue isn't which to save first, a human or an animal, but whether a human can *kill* an animal, for trivial or serious reasons. Bella and Edward's shared ethic says reasons matter. Bella could not take up hunting and run through the woods killing deer for their taste, but Edward can, for survival. It's the same deer, though. How can the different reasons Bella and Edward would have for hunting switch the deer's rights on and off? It sounds like magic!

If you approach moral questions within the framework of Utilitarianism—an influential moral theory developed in the nineteenth century—then you don't actually have to answer this question.[3] You're not going to think about moral issues in terms of rights to begin with. The prime directive, for a Utilitarian, is to maximize the balance of happiness over misery, taking into account all individuals who can feel happiness or misery. Animals clearly count, since they can feel these emotions. If Bella's reason for eating venison were merely the pleasure of taste, the loss of a deer's future pleasures would not be offset by what she gained. But if Edward's reason for killing a deer is survival, then the loss of a deer's future pleasures probably *is* offset by what he gains, since it seems probable that his life is packed with more pleasure than a deer's.

Case closed, maybe. But Utilitarianism is a moral theory with a variety of serious problems. In any case, when we talk about moral issues, rights talk is our native language. So let's get back to the question about the deer's rights: Do they magically switch on and off depending on a prospective hunter's reasons for killing?

A right is nothing overly grand and complicated, as I am using the term. To have rights is merely for there to be limits on how you can be treated, due to your own nature. To have rights is *not* to be a mere thing, to be stepped on, chopped up, punched, or pureed to the satisfaction of others. An absolute right protects absolutely—against all intrusions. The reasons of the potential intruder make no difference. But we don't often think of rights as being absolute—not even human rights. Yes, we have a right to free speech, but we can be silenced if we're yelling "Fire!" in a movie theater or inciting a riot.

An individual has rights against being harmed or exploited due to attributes that call forth respect. Some philosophers have an extremely narrow view of the attributes that command respect. Immanuel Kant (1724–1804), the great eighteenth-century German philosopher, viewed the capacity for morality as the only one that deserves respect. Since animals don't have that capacity, he thought, animals don't deserve any respect, and we can do literally anything to them, so long as our behavior doesn't have any repercussions for other human beings.

Tom Regan, a leading contemporary animal rights advocate, takes a position at the other extreme; he says the very same respect is owed to every "subject of a life." Thus, we can no more kill animals to meet our needs than we can kill other human beings. In his view, you apparently wouldn't even be warranted in killing a deer to save your life, except in the unlikely event you were being attacked by one. As Regan puts it, animals are not our "resources."[4] Period.

To my mind, Kant and Regan are both wrong. It's more plausible that respect is the proper response to many things— sheer consciousness, intelligence, reflectiveness, the sense of self, artistic ability, athletic ability, the capacity for morality, to name a few. But some individuals have more respect-worthy traits than others. All due respect is just a little respect in some cases and a lot of respect in others. If rights are stronger and weaker depending on what there is to respect in an individual, then animals may have rights, but they are weaker than our own.

The stronger the right, the more that an individual wears a "keep out" sign, and our reasons for wanting to use him or her for some purpose are powerless to justify intrusion. The weaker the right, the more that our reasons can make a difference. But what counts as a strong reason? What makes some reasons strong, and others weak?

We can also do some of our thinking about the strength of reasons in terms of respect. Bella may like the taste of venison, but is that a strong reason to end the life of a deer? Well, would it cost Bella any self-respect to forgo it? Would she feel diminished? I should think not.

But now suppose Edward must have a blood meal. If he abstains from blood out of respect for animals and allows himself to wither away, he surely would be lacking in self-respect. He'd be giving too much credit to the animals he spares, and too little to himself—considering that he is in fact a more complex and respect-worthy being.

So—quod erat demonstrandum—Edward may consume deer, but Bella may not. And neither can have a human meal.

Scene 2. In Which a Classmate Brings Up an Unpleasant Scenario

If Edward and Bella say all this, they'll give their classmates plenty to chew on. I suspect, though, that some thoughtful classmate is going to start imagining a problematic hypothetical scenario.

First, an observation about the *Twilight* series. Isn't it convenient that Edward cannot survive without a blood meal but doesn't specifically need to suck the blood of a human being? Without that peculiarity, the *Twilight* series would be kaput. A boy who goes around killing people, even for purposes of survival, isn't a suitable companion for a teenage girl.

Had the story been told that way, the books wouldn't have been so successful, but they'd be awfully interesting, from an ethical point of view. Would an Edward who needs to consume human blood be able to defend the traditional vampire diet in terms of *our* rights being overridable?

Quite possibly he and other vampires would think so. First they'd stress the difference between vampires and humans. They have the power to live forever, which is something we can only dream of. We are continually trying to lengthen our life spans through medicine, and our Western religions portray everlasting life as the ultimate reward for a life lived well. But live for centuries, or even forever, *here*? We can't do it.

Vampires also seem to have all sorts of extra mental and physical abilities. Some can see the future, others can fly. We can do neither. Edward and his kin might claim that they must suck our blood, out of self-respect and in light of the fact that our rights are overridden by their need to survive. It would be no different from the situation in the books, where

Edward is entitled to eat deer to survive. His reasons trump their rights; in the very same way, his reasons in the alternative *Twilight* would trump our rights.

But this doesn't sound right. Surely it's a far more problematic thing for man-eating Edward to kill one of us than for vegetarian Edward to eat a deer. Isn't it?

Maybe what's going on here is that both vampires and people exceed a threshold, so that both races enjoy an extremely strong right to life, not one to be trumped by another person's survival problems. Since they both have enough capacities to make it past this threshold, the difference between their capacities is immaterial.

Try using this argument on a famished vampire. I think you might start hearing him or her talk just like we would about deer. "Sure, you mere humans have some rights, but our serious reasons take precedence." It would be advisable to have a backup argument, if you expected to make it through the debate with all of your blood in your veins. In fact, there really *is* more to vampires killing people, and seeing the additional issues sheds light on how *our* relationship to animals differs from our relationship to other people.

To see the difference, we need to borrow a few basic ideas from the social contract tradition in ethics and political philosophy—the tradition founded by Thomas Hobbes (1588–1679) in the sixteenth century and John Locke (1632–1704) in the seventeenth. The social contract philosophers contrasted the state of nature and the state of living together as a society, under laws. In a state of nature, each individual is on his own, looking out for his own interests. When one individual looks at another, he looks at "just" another and not at a fellow member of one community. That doesn't necessarily mean "anything goes." Locke thought that even in the state of nature, individuals have certain rights. There are already limits on what they can do to each other. But they don't live together in a law-governed society.

When we encounter an animal, we find ourselves in a state of nature with respect to that animal. We are not members of the same community. (I'm ignoring laws that regulate the treatment of animals, but they are very weak anyway. I'm also ignoring the complicated topic of relationships with pets.) Again it's not "anything goes." As humans have natural rights even in the state of nature, it makes sense to think animals do, too. With or without an enveloping community, there is much about an animal that deserves to be respected, and there are limits on what we can do to animals. At the very least, we must leave animals alone to live their lives, unless we have very good reasons to intrude and use an animal for our purposes.

For our interactions with animals, the state of nature is more or less permanent. It's never going to be the case that animals are exactly fellow citizens. But with humans, the state of nature is something long gone, if it ever really existed to begin with. We live within communities, under rules that we implicitly agree to. One rule we agree to is that everybody gets to have an equal right to life. Nobody gets to eat anybody else, even in a life-and-death situation. The Einsteins and Picassos among us don't get to eat the incapacitated or even the extremely incapacitated. But why? Why, especially, should the Einsteins and Picassos agree to such rules?

They agree for very deep-seated biological and emotional reasons, to be sure, but also because of the psychology of being a community member with concerns about the future. You may see yourself as one of the lucky ones today, but anybody's susceptible to an ability-reducing disease or accident. And even if you retain all of your present capacities, there's no telling when others will *perceive* you as less able.

Aside from worries about our personal fate, we all also have to worry about the fate of our children and our parents, who could be severely disabled. And then, there's considerable empathy even between strangers that would make us suffer if we knew people were being eaten, even if we weren't personally affected. As members of a community, we would set up rules that make sense over the long term and protect us and those we care about even as the roles and status of different individuals may shift over time. We certainly wouldn't permit eating one another, even for survival purposes.

In *Twilight* there's a band of murderous vampires who live in a sort of state of nature. They roam around killing humans merely because they're so tasty. They violate even the very basic morality that exists outside the confines of a community. If Edward had to kill to survive, maybe (just maybe) he could make the case that his reasons override our rights, and so he wouldn't violate the primitive morality of the state of nature, but he'd certainly stop being a true member of our community. He'd have to skulk around in the shadows, keeping secrets and telling lies.

And that would be extremely unfortunate for him. The Cullens need and want to be a part of our community. They can't live happily as skulking creatures of darkness. Had Stephenie Meyer imagined Edward as needing human blood for survival, there would have been a dilemma at the heart of the books that couldn't be resolved. Survive as an outlaw or die as one of us? That would have been the question.

The bottom line is the way we think about killing animals can't be transposed into the key of killing people. When vampires contemplate killing people (or people contemplate killing people) new issues come into play. It makes a difference that other people are fellow citizens, while animals are not.

Scene 3. In Which Edward Says No to the Kosher Option

Luckily for Edward, Bella, and the *Twilight* series, Edward only needs to kill animals, not humans, to survive. Or so I've been assuming. Some attentive student is bound to press

Edward on this: "Who says you must kill animals for food? You can't survive without a blood meal, but that doesn't mean you need to kill animals. You could partially drain the blood of a couple of deer, and let them all survive!"

I think Edward's going to make faces at this point, and probably become a little menacing. What he'll remind the challenger is that it is excruciatingly difficult for a vampire to stop midway through a blood meal. Fine, we know that. But if that's the reason Edward kills animals, let's be precise about it. The blood is necessary for his survival, but the killing is not; it's really just a strong preference. Is that enough to warrant killing animals?

Edward may want to back away from that question by insisting there's another reason for him to suck the life out of animals. In the *Twilight* cosmos, bad things happen to partially drained animals. They limp away in permanent pain. Edward's not just an out-of-control animal devouring other animals; he hunts animals to the death because he's made a judgment that this is the right thing to do.

As long as we've invented a college in Forks, let's also invent a kosher butcher shop. In the Bible it says that the blood of an animal must not be eaten, "because the blood is the life" (Deuteronomy 12:23). So animals slaughtered in the kosher fashion are completely drained of their blood. (Vampires, being consumers of blood, obviously don't keep kosher.) Now, as long as there's all that blood being spilled, why not let someone use it? (And yes, kosher meat processors do sell "treif" animal by-products to nonobservant customers instead of throwing them away.) If the Cullens bought their blood meals from the kosher butcher, they could keep themselves alive without any more animal death and suffering than there already is.

Right. I very much doubt the Cullens would want to be customers of the kosher butcher. If they had to say why, maybe they'd have to own up to a fondness for killing. Killing is what vampires do—it is at the core of their being. Maybe it's an essential species characteristic—like hunting is to lions. Vampires are built for the task, as their teeth demonstrate. Or maybe we should see vampires as sharing a common culture. Completely draining an animal's blood is culturally central, like whaling is for Eskimos. So killing animals may not be crucial for Edward's physical survival, but it's central to his survival as the individual he is.

These are reasons for killing that go beyond simple taste, but are they serious enough? We've seen a defense of killing animals for survival in these pages and an attack on killing them just for their taste. But there are lots of reasons that lie between those two extremes. Can we go on killing animals to provide the turkey that's central for Thanksgiving, the hot dogs that are part of watching a baseball game, the lobster that makes a trip to Maine a trip to Maine? Can we kill just to perpetuate the lifestyle and the relationship to nature we're accustomed to? Can we kill for any reason short of survival?

We need to be wary of rationalizations that masquerade as deep, existential reasons, but it's fair to say there are difficult questions here. Once it's granted that ending a life *is* a serious matter, we do need to discuss what counts as a good enough reason. No doubt the class stayed late to discuss the matter, far into the night.

And then they all went home hungry, Bella to have a late-night vegetarian snack with her dad, and Edward to the forest.[5]

NOTES

1. See Singer's reply to J. M. Coetzee in *The Lives of Animals* (Princeton, NJ: Princeton University Press, 1999), pp. 85–91. See also Peter Singer, *Animal Liberation* (New York: Ecco, 2002), pp. 1–23.

2. I defend this approach against others in my book, *Animalkind: What We Owe to the Animals*, chap. 5 (Hoboken, NJ: Wiley-Blackwell, forthcoming January 2010). All of the ideas about ethics and animals in this essay are further explored there.

3. For Utilitarian perspectives on meat-eating, see chapters 9 and 10 of the very useful anthology *Food for Thought: The Debate Over Eating Meat* (Amherst, NY: Prometheus, 2004). pp. 118–137.

4. See Tom Regan and Peter Singer, *Animal Rights and Human Obligations* (New York: Prentice-Hall, 1989), pp. 105–114.

5. Thank you to Becky Groves for introducing me to the *Twilight* world and correcting my mistakes about the way it works, and to Peter Groves for feedback and good ideas.

CAN A VAMPIRE BE A PERSON?

Nicolas Michaud

Edward Cullen is a loving husband, a brilliant musician, a devoted son, and a remarkable baseball player. But of course, Edward is also a vampire. Do you need to be human to be a person? What are the criteria for personhood? This chapter will address whether you have to be human to be called a "person," or whether vampires like Edward and the Cullens have more "personhood" than the rest of us.

A person is simply a bearer of rights, someone worthy of respect. Being a human does not automatically make you a person. Sadly, society has often not treated women and minorities as persons. So being human has not always been used as part of the criteria for personhood. For instance, intelligent extraterrestrials could potentially be persons, and some animal rights advocates argue that animals are persons as well.

Twilight's vampires, though human in appearance, are significantly different from most humans. They are nearly immortal and do not age; they are super-strong and super-fast. Beyond that, vampires have super senses; they can smell scents humans cannot, hear a human heartbeat from miles away, and see details so fine that a human would need a microscope to match such vision.

Perhaps due to their immortality, vampires take a very different view of how they should live life. Most do not act as if human lives need preservation and see human beings simply as food. Vampires are often portrayed as vastly superior to human beings, in part because of their physical superiority, but also because of their mental superiority. Vampires have tremendous clarity of mind and incredible memories, among other gifts. As a result, most vampires have very different ethical outlooks. Whereas humans are normally concerned with the needs and feelings of others, vampires are often solitary creatures not even concerned with one another's welfare. There's simply no need.

What Is a Person (Other Than Vampire Food)?

The philosopher Immanuel Kant (1724–1804) argued that being a human was not enough to make you a person. Instead, rationality, the ability to think, makes someone a person. We might wonder, what about computers? No one thinks we have to show respect for our computers or treat them with dignity. Despite their processing powers, we don't count computers as part of the moral community.

To clarify, for Kant, being a person did not simply mean being "rational." It meant "being part of the moral community." To be part of the moral community means that because of your rationality you deserve to be treated as if you have rights; you deserve respect and dignity. Rocks clearly are not part of the moral community, but other cases are not quite as obvious.

The contemporary philosopher Mary Anne Warren asks us to imagine meeting a nonhuman being. We need to ask ourselves, "What qualities would a being possess to make humans consider that being a part of the moral community?" Warren argues that there are five qualities that would indicate whom we should treat with respect: (1) consciousness, (2) reasoning, (3) self-motivated activity, (4) the capacity to communicate, and (5) the presence of self-concepts.[1]

Warren doesn't believe that a being must have all of these characteristics to be treated as a person, but at least a combination of several is necessary, usually involving numbers one and three. For example, if I run into a being that is conscious and demonstrates self-motivated activity, even if it lacks the ability to commutate with me I would still treat it as if it deserves some rights.

Warren helps us realize how little importance *should be* placed on the biological difference between vampires and humans. *Twilight*'s vampires meet all five criteria. To say that they are not persons simply because they are physically different from us amounts to arbitrary speciesism. Tom Regan, a contemporary philosopher who defends animal rights, offers the following in response to those who deny animals rights simply because animals are not human:

> There are those who resist the idea that animals have inherent value. "Only humans have such value," they profess. How might this narrow view be defended? Shall we say that only humans have the requisite intelligence, or autonomy, or reason? But there are many, many humans who fail to meet these standards and yet are reasonably viewed as having value beyond their usefulness to others. Shall we claim that only humans belong to the right species, the species Homo sapiens? But this is blatant speciesism.[2]

Is there any legitimate basis for rejecting Regan? As Regan mentions, almost any criterion, other than "they aren't human," is one that humans can lack. For example, many very young children are not intelligent at all; in fact, an adult gorilla may be smarter than a young child. Why is it that we have to treat the child with respect and not the gorilla? It seems that the only answer we have is that the gorilla isn't human, but of course, *neither is Edward*. Does that mean we should treat Edward the way that we treat animals? It's easy to say that being human is necessary for respect when we want to eat the tastier animals or put exotic or attractive animals in cages for our enjoyment, but it becomes much more complex when we realize that other nonhumans, like Edward, may deserve to be part of the moral community.

What Humans, Vampires, and Animals Have in Common

Let's consider a very different perspective on how we *should* treat others. Contemporary philosopher Martha Nussbaum doesn't argue about how we can tell if something is a person as much as how we can tell if something has particular capabilities. If it has the capability for reason, for example, we shouldn't interfere with that capability. Instead of arguing that Edward is intelligent and therefore he is a person, Nussbaum takes a simpler approach. She would say Edward is capable of reason, and so we should let him use his reason. In other words, if something has the capability to do something that doesn't harm anyone else, why interfere with it?

Nussbaum provides us with a list of capabilities that are of central importance as a necessity for a fulfilling and happy life—what she calls "flourishing." In order for you to flourish, a capability isn't something you must fulfill, it's just something others shouldn't interfere with if you seek that fulfillment. Nussbaum argues that human beings have ten central capabilities:[3]

1. Life—the ability to live to the end of a life of normal length.

2. Bodily health—the ability to have good health.
3. Bodily integrity—the ability to be secure from violence and move as we choose.
4. Senses, imagination, and thought—the ability to use the senses, to imagine, think, and reason.
5. Emotions—the ability to have attachments to things and people outside ourselves.
6. Practical reason—the ability to engage in critical reflection.
7. Affiliation—the ability to live with and toward others and have self-respect.
8. Other species—the ability to live with concern for animals, plants, and nature.
9. Play—the ability to enjoy recreational activities.
10. Control over one's environment—the ability to participate in politics and hold property.

The idea is that we should not interfere with someone else's capabilities on Nussbaum's list, because those capabilities are necessary in order to flourish. We have other capabilities not listed as central to flourishing, for example, the capability to kill. Nussbaum lists two reasons for this: (1) because it is not necessary for flourishing, and (2) because it interferes with the capabilities of others to flourish.

Nussbaum's list doesn't determine who should count as a person, but it does determine rights and dignities that should be granted to those who have what she terms central capabilities. For example, the capability *life* does not make something a person, but those who have it shouldn't be denied it. If we used Nussbaum's capabilities list as a way of determining how we should treat others, it is unlikely anything would be mistreated. This is important, because not all people we consider to be persons today have always been treated as persons. Notoriously, early U.S. law considered slaves to be three-fifths of a person; women were not even given the right to vote until 1920. Had Nussbaum's capabilities list been followed, African Americans and others would not have been kept as slaves, and women would not have had to fight for the better part of a century to earn rights such as the vote.

If we used Nussbaum's list, we likely would grant Edward all of the rights humans enjoy so as to not interfere with his capabilities. But the careful reader will notice that the capabilities also seem to apply to animals. Nussbaum realizes this herself and argues that animals should be granted certain rights based on their capabilities, like the rest of us.[4] Animals should not be slaughtered for food, used for scientific testing, or mistreated in any way that denies animals flourishing lives. But let's look at it from another perspective.

If Animals Are Human Food, Are We Vampire Food?

Rather than accept Nussbaum's conclusion, you might simply ask, why not deny Edward personhood? After all, Edward is not human, and as noted earlier, he is *very* different. But why should difference matter? In many ways vampires are *superior* to humans. The very reasoning used to deny animals personhood would quickly work against us. The main reason animals are denied personhood is that animal intelligence and communication are different from that of humans. But the Volturi could argue the same thing regarding us. They are smarter, they are capable of doing many things we can only dream about, and if they chose to herd us like cattle into pens for the slaughter, they could with ease (and do, in the case of some rather unfortunate tourists). So on what basis do we say humans deserve special treatment in the face of nonhumans who can do everything better?

There is only one argument that counts us as persons to physically superior vampires: humans have souls. This makes us special. And in *Twilight* the soul is important; Edward even fears he has lost his and worries that Bella may lose hers, too, when she becomes a vampire.

But there's a larger problem with the assumption that humans are special because of our souls: How do you know you have one? How do you test for a soul? Souls are a matter more of faith than of fact; there is no test *ever* that could confirm a soul's existence. So how can we say that vampires don't have souls? Imagine that a vampire argued that *humans* don't have souls! How would we prove that vampire wrong? Vampires could argue that proof of their souls is in their superiority over humans. The vampire might argue that if humans had souls, God wouldn't make them so easy to kill. (This is exactly the argument we often use against animals.)

There's another issue here, too. Let's say we could prove that we *do* have souls. Why should this matter? After all, human beings have many features that make us unique, but that have no weight whatsoever when thinking about morality. Humans are the only animals that make pizza, or buy stocks, or wage war. This hardly makes us better, morally speaking, than other animals. So what's so great about this soul thing?

We can't really use biology or souls to distinguish between a person and a nonperson, and this may mean that animals should also be granted a kind of personhood. The alternative in both the biological and the soul cases is to allow vampires the possibility of treating us as nonpersons because of their biological "superiority" to humans and our inability to prove who does, and who does not, have a soul. So instead I'd argue that Warren, Regan, and Nussbaum are all on to something. Personhood should be granted to those who demonstrate certain qualities such as consciousness and self-motivated activity; those who demonstrate certain capabilities such as practical reason and affiliation should also not be denied the ability to flourish if they so choose.

Naughty Vampire! No People for You!

Recall that sometimes we don't grant that a certain human is a person. It might be because of arbitrary and bigoted reasons (we want to keep slaves) or because we believe that personhood requires certain ethical notions (notions a serial killer lacks, for example). Vampires often act in ways that we consider horribly unethical. If a person rejects the morals of the community in drastic ways that violate the personhood of others, then they themselves choose to be apart from the moral community, and thereby choose to stand outside the moral realm of persons.

This is different from the case of animals who cannot determine that they want to reject morality; they simply do not understand it. Animals are then objects of our moral treatment, though they couldn't choose to participate fully in the moral community. Animals would thus have a limited kind of personhood. We wouldn't grant them the right to vote, nor would we expect them to treat us with dignity. But we also should not eat them by virtue of Nussbaum's capabilities list, because animals can be persons whose capabilities we respect. But we wouldn't ask them to vote or serve on juries, because animals lack the capacity for such tasks. Their inability to participate fully, however, is crucially unlike the serial killer, who *chooses* to reject the moral community and the capabilities of others.

One might argue that vampires are serial killers. Most choose to reject conventional morality and exit the community. The Cullens, however, do not subscribe to the Volturi ethical system, so we cannot lump the Cullens together with the serial killer clan. This suggests a general policy for humans and vampires alike: Moral personhood may be judged only on a case-by-case basis. Each vampire should be judged as a participant in the moral community as an individual. We would reject, punish, or in the case of the Volturi, defend ourselves from those who choose to violate the personhood and capabilities of others.

The great irony, though, is this: If we choose to reject some individuals as nonpersons because of their willingness to harm others, we may find ourselves as only partial persons. Why? If by our accounts animals have a kind of limited personhood, then our treatment of them is analogous to the Volturi's treatment of us. So if the Volturi should be punished or denied personhood because of their treatment of other persons, then we should similarly be punished for our treatment of these other weaker animal-persons. In the end Edward might be not only a person, but a better person than most humans. After all, he refrains from killing those who are weaker and less intelligent than he is, while humans gladly kill animals weaker with different intelligences.

Stephenie Meyer's use of "vegetarian" vampires in her *Twilight* saga leaves great philosophical space to explore issues such as how we define personhood. Now that you know the criteria, are you worthy of being a person? It may not be as easy a question to answer as you think.

NOTES

1. Mary Anne Warren, "On the Moral and Legal Status of Abortion," *Monist* 57:1, 43–61 (1973).

2. Thomas Regan, *The Case for Animal Rights* (Berkeley: University of California Press, 2004).

3. Martha Nussbaum and Amartya Sen, *The Quality of Life* (Oxford, UK: Clarendon Press, 1993).

4. Martha Nussbaum and Cass Sunstien (eds.), *Animal Rights: Current Debates and New Directions* (Oxford: Oxford University Press, 2004).

four

CARLISLE: MORE COMPASSIONATE THAN A SPEEDING BULLET?

Andrew Terjesen and Jenny Terjesen

Aside from super-speed, super-strength, super-senses, and immortality, quite a few of the vampires in the *Twilight* series have their own personal special abilities, what the Cullens call "gifts." Aro, leader of the Volturi, surrounds himself with these extra-powerful vampires, "collecting" them and their abilities. Edward Cullen reads minds, while Alice Cullen sees possible futures. And when Bella Swan is turned into a vampire, she learns she can shield against other vampires' mental abilities, even Aro's. Carlisle Cullen's gift is quite different from the rest: his gift seems to be compassion. But what does that mean? How is caring about people the same as reading minds or seeing the future? In what way would Carlisle's compassion set him apart from either humans or other vampires?

There's definitely something special about Carlisle. His dedication to his "vegetarian" lifestyle and his accomplishment in creating a vampire family that also follows his dietetic choice are quite remarkable. But does Carlisle have some special gift that other vampires lack? Or is he just a very good person? Many philosophers have argued that compassion is at the heart of being a good person. So maybe it isn't too far-fetched that Carlisle's super-compassion is what makes it possible for him to do something that no other vampire before him had been able to do.

Carlisle's Theory of "Gifts"

Over mushroom ravioli, Edward relates to Bella Carlisle's theory about vampiric gifts: "[W]e all bring something of our strongest human traits with us into the next life, where they are intensified—like our minds, and our senses."[1] According to Carlisle's theory, even as a human being, Edward was very sensitive to thoughts of people around him, and Alice probably had some sort of precognition before she was turned.

It's an interesting theory, but is there any evidence that it's true? Actually, there is. We know a lot about Bella's gift before she became a vampire. One of the first things that attracts Edward's attention to Bella is that he cannot read her thoughts. Later on, in *New Moon*, she proves resistant to Jane's pain whammy. Bella wonders if this just makes her a freak. It turns out that it does, but in a cool way.

Bella is a very private, shy person who hides her thoughts and feelings. But her protectiveness extends further than her own comfort and safety to those she cares about. Her concern for others is reflected, for example, when she talks about her relationship with Edward: "Edward was worried about the time we'd spent together publicly . . . if things went wrong. I refused to dwell on the last thought, concentrating instead on making things safer for him."[2]

We clearly see Bella's willingness to do anything she can to protect others at the end of *Twilight*, when she goes on a suicide mission in order to save Renee. She knows that trying to save Renee will probably get her killed, but she doesn't let that deter her from walking right into James's trap. If there is anything Bella can do to protect those she cares about, she will do it. In light of all this, it really does seem that Bella's "shield" is an intensification of the most definitive aspect of her character. As a vampire, she's finally empowered to cast her shield on those she cares about to protect them from the harmful mental abilities of the Volturi.

Carlisle's Super-Compassion

Edward says that "Carlisle brought his compassion" from his human life. He's literally bloodthirsty, but he's a teetotaler. As a vampire doctor caring for humans, he's like an alcoholic working as a bartender. It's dangerous, but he's really good at it, complete with an excellent bedside manner that puts patients at ease. But is that really a "super-power?"

Consider Carlisle's compassion and control in extreme situations. Bella's birthday party paper cut thrusts Jasper Cullen into feeding frenzy mode. The terrible cuts Bella gets from the mirror at the end of *Twilight* start to erode the control of all the Cullens except Carlisle. Even Edward has to step away while Carlisle stitches her up.

In *Midnight Sun*, we get a possible glimpse into Carlisle's head through Edward's "gift."[3] When Carlisle is treating Bella's head injury, Edward says, "I ached for the difference between Carlisle and me—that he could touch her so gently, without fear, knowing he would never harm her."[4] In Edward's narration, we see that Carlisle really has mastered his bloodlust.

The Denali clan, who are also vegetarians, keep themselves largely removed from human affairs. Their decision

not to feed on humans seems driven more by rational calcula-
tion than by the affection for humanity that Carlisle displays.
Moreover, while Carlisle never forces his own choice on his
friends or family, he seems to inspire it in them. Edward is
the first vampire Carlisle makes, and while Edward never
doubts Carlisle's sincerity in believing his abstention is the
right path, he doesn't accept that as truth right away, either.
For a decade or so he feeds on the blood of evil men, until he
comes to the conclusion that Carlisle is right.

As far as we know, Carlisle has never drunk human blood.
When he became a vampire, he was so distraught that he
tried to kill himself a number of ways, including starvation,
until he discovered he could survive on animal blood. Even
the Volturi could not pressure him into drinking human
blood, though he admired them for their civility and culture.
His compassion allows him to stick to his pledge and sets him
apart from other vampires.

Is Compassion a Feeling?

If Carlisle's gift is what enables him to resist the urge to kill
humans, it would be really helpful if we could understand
it better. Since vampiric gifts are based on human traits, it
would seem that Stephenie Meyer is exploring the idea that
there is a human trait that inhibits violent action—a trait
that we would want all people to develop, if they could.

For a lot of people, compassion is a feeling we get when
we see something bad happening. Consider the Chinese philosopher Mencius (371–289 BCE), who said we all have a
"sprout" of compassion, by which he meant that we are all
born with a very general feeling of concern for others.

> The reason why I say that humans all have hearts that
> will not bear the suffering of others is this. Suppose
> someone suddenly saw a child about to fall into a well:

everyone in such a situation would have a feeling of alarm and compassion—not because one sought to get in good with the child's parents, not because one wanted fame among their neighbors and friends, and not because one would dislike the sound of the child's cries.[5]

Mencius called this feeling a "sprout" because it is not fully developed. Rather, it needs to be nurtured and grown into the virtue of caring for everyone all the time. Without such nurturing, compassion is limited to babies, puppies, and of course, the people we care about. It doesn't stretch any farther.

Think of the limited compassion of Tanya's clan. They care for the human men that they frolic with, so they don't harm them. But their feelings don't reach any farther. Lacking compassion, Tanya and the Denali clan determine it is not in their self-interest to help Carlisle's family defend against Victoria's newborn army in *Eclipse*. In *Breaking Dawn*, they are willing to side with the Cullens partly out of guilt for not helping before and partly out of concern for Renesmee's safety and right to live. (And maybe because they feel a little bad about Irina flying off the handle and bringing the Volturi down on the Cullens' heads.) Tanya's feelings are linked to specific things. But her feelings for Renesmee and Carlisle's family wouldn't be enough to generate the kind of self-control that Carlisle exhibits in the hospital.

So one problem with thinking of compassion as just a feeling is that people's feelings are different and often capricious. After all, if Renesmee were the one to fall down the well, the Volturi would not be alarmed at all—nor would anyone who thought she was an "immortal child." Another problem with defining compassion as a feeling is reflected in Mencius's baby-falling-down-the-well example. Mencius only said that we would feel alarm when we see the baby fall down the well, but he never said that we would do anything about it. Our feelings do not always move us to action. One could be a vampire, like Edward, who feeds on humans and feels bad about it (the fact that they are evil humans doesn't change that much), but his feelings don't stop him from feeding. At least, it's not his feelings alone that cause him to adopt Carlisle's diet.

Compassion of a Saint?

So Mencius's notion of compassion as a feeling that crops up in certain circumstances does not capture what makes Carlisle special. Perhaps it is a different notion of compassion that is at work here. In the Buddhist tradition, compassion refers to our concern for all living things. So it's not a specific feeling that arises only in certain circumstances, such as when babies are in danger. Instead it is something that applies to all circumstances. The Dalai Lama describes compassion in the following way: "True compassion is not just an emotional response but a firm commitment founded on reason. . . . For a Buddhist practitioner, the goal is to develop this genuine compassion, this genuine wish for the well-being of another, in fact for every living being throughout the universe."[6]

Compassion understood as universal rational concern seems much more promising, as it reflects Carlisle's concern. His "vegetarianism" shows his reluctance to kill humans in order to sate his hunger, but he also seems unwilling to kill them for other reasons. In fact, he seems to think that saving a life can be more important than the life he has created with his family. In the *Midnight Sun* draft, Carlisle tells Edward he did the right thing when he saved Bella, even though stopping the car risked exposing his vampiric nature (and all of the other Cullens as well). Throughout the series, Carlisle tries to avoid violence in order to avoid unnecessary death. And he puts himself in the middle of a smorgasbord of human blood in order to save lives on a daily basis.

Is this Carlisle's super-compassion—the belief that all living things should be treated well? Before we jump to that conclusion, we need to consider where that belief comes from. Carlisle's gift would not be the belief itself; it would be whatever makes it possible for him to hold that belief (what the Dalai Lama calls a "firm commitment") when so many others don't. The Buddhist notion of compassion grows out of the idea that all life is suffering. Even when we are not in physical pain or emotional anguish, we are not perfectly at ease in the world. So the reason I should treat all people well is that, like me, they are suffering.

The philosopher Arthur Schopenhauer (1788–1860) also held to an ethics of compassion. Schopenhauer's reason for promoting compassion was that once you understood the nature of the world, you would realize that the individual is a very insignificant part of that world. Schopenhauer saw compassion as the logical response to a world in which particular individuals were not so important that their desires should triumph over everyone else's. Once we see what makes this notion of compassion possible, we must recognize that this couldn't be what is going on in Carlisle. He created a family, and that family is very important to him. It's unthinkable that his gift would be rooted in the idea that his family is not any more important than any other family. Plus, while he doesn't kill humans for food, he doesn't believe that every person has an equal right to life (since he accepts Rosalie's actions in Rochester, for example). And of course, he does kill animals for food, even though he could conceivably live on human blood from blood banks. So there must be some other notion of compassion—between the poles of particular feelings and all-encompassing concern—that captures Carlisle's gift.

Compassion, Caring, and the Cullen Family

Edward tells Bella Carlisle's story early on in their relationship, and so we learn that Carlisle didn't have much of a family when he was human. His mother died during his birth, and his father was an Anglican pastor more concerned with stamping out witchery and demons than with being a good dad. Of course, he wasn't as good at catching actual witches and vampires as he probably was at pointing fingers and getting innocent people condemned for being such. But Carlisle obviously felt a duty to please his father, because he obeyed and took charge of the raids once his father was too old to continue them himself. Unlike his father, Carlisle was not able to help the Church convict innocent people of being monsters. No, Carlisle went out and found an actual monster. He found a real coven of vampires. And that, as they say, is all she wrote.

So when Carlisle awoke to find himself one of his father's reviled monsters, he was pretty upset. But he didn't take that out on people around him or give in to the extreme thirst for blood. Instead, he removed himself from populated areas, and when he was overcome with thirst he preyed on deer. Thus vampire "vegetarianism" was born.

So Carlisle figures he can live with himself if he doesn't kill people to do it, and he sets out to make something of himself, studying and traveling and becoming a doctor, of all things, and meeting other vampires, like the famous Volturi. And none of these vampires get it. (Carlisle might as well have a red shiny nose.) He's a lonely guy. But Carlisle keeps on going, all the way to the New World. That's when he finds Edward in the middle of the influenza epidemic and makes the promise to "save him." Suddenly Carlisle has a son, a brother, a comrade. But he never changes anyone who might have a chance to live out a human life.

Throughout his life and his unlife, Carlisle tries to connect with other people. The idea that compassion is a kind of reciprocal connection that we form with others is found in a philosophical tradition known as "care ethics." According to care ethics, our relationships to other people constitute the bedrock of all moral thinking. The Cullens are not a family by virtue of blood (or even blood-drinking). They are a family because they share relationships with one another that define not only who they are, but how they live their lives.

The contemporary philosopher Michael Slote describes compassion as "empathy-based caring."[7] By this definition, Carlisle's compassion is his ability to care for people after he forms a relationship that enables him to connect with them and understand how they feel. That sounds like the Carlisle we know! The advantage of this definition of compassion is that it captures the importance of Carlisle's particular relations to the rest of the Cullens. His deeper relationship to his family means that he is obligated to do more for them. This obligation, though, can be transferred to other people through his existing relationships. So, for example, because he cares about Edward and Edward cares about Bella, that means Carlisle now has an important relationship with Bella.

But how does this explain Carlisle's ability to resist feeding on strangers? Here, too, care ethics has an answer. The contemporary philosopher Nel Noddings, in her book *Caring*, argues, "When the relation has not yet been established, or when it may properly be refused . . . the imperative is more like that of the hypothetical: I must if I wish to (or am able to) move into relation."[8] So according to care ethics, every person we meet is someone we could enter into a relationship with. Out of respect for the possible relationship, there are some basic rules we must follow—the most important one, for vampires, being "don't eat me."

The Power of Connections

At the end of *Breaking Dawn*, Garrett gives a rousing speech:

> I came here at Carlisle's request, as the others, to witness. . . . I stayed to witness something else. You. . . .

These ancient ones did *not* come here for justice as they told you. . . . The Volturi come to erase what they perceive as the competition. Perhaps, like me, you look at this clan's golden eyes and marvel. They are difficult to understand, it's true. But the ancient ones look and see something besides their strange choice. They see *power*.[9]

The Volturi did not build their clan on the connections that the Cullens formed as a family. Instead they used fear and punishment to keep everything "civilized." As Garrett points out, however, the Cullens have found a different kind of power that the Volturi cannot contain. Garrett goes on to testify that he's studied the family and it's clear to him

that intrinsic to this intense family binding—that which makes them possible at all—is the peaceful character of this life of sacrifice. There is no aggression here like we all saw in the large southern clans that grew and diminished so quickly in their wild feuds. There is no thought for domination. And Aro knows this better than I do. . . . I came to witness. I stay to fight. The Volturi care nothing for the death of the child. They seek the death of our free will.[10]

Political nonviolent protest threatens the status quo that keeps the Volturi in power. It's like Gandhi all over again. That's a superpower worth mentioning.

As further evidence of the power of caring connections to make people act more responsibly, consider Jasper's connection to Alice, which helped to inhibit his bloodlust even before he joined the Cullens. Nor is the connection limited to the immediate family. The Denali's encounter with Carlisle and ensuing relationship is what sets the Denali clan on their path toward a different lifestyle. In *Midnight Sun*, Edward talks about how he wanted to kill those potential rapists in Port Angeles, and Carlisle thinks, "She's very good for you, isn't she? So much compassion, so much control."[11] Edward's relationship to Bella helps him to control his violent impulses, and presumably Carlisle's extraordinary ability to relate to everyone helps him to control his vampiric impulses to an unprecedented degree.

The best example of this, though, is Renesmee's power. Carlisle jokes that Renesmee's power to project her thoughts into other peoples' minds and inspire a desire to protect are a flip of both Bella's and Edward's gifts. But Renesmee also cements Carlisle's alliance of witnesses to stand with him against the Volturi. In that sense Renesmee also seems to have a bit of her "grandfather" in her, so to speak. She creates connections almost immediately with Tanya and others. Those connections make them want to take care of her, even if it means facing off against the Volturi.

Since Carlisle can overcome some of the most destructive desires imaginable, it only makes sense that his ability to do so is a gift. We have several examples in the *Twilight* series that show the power of a genuine emotional connection to overcome selfish and destructive desires. We are drawn then to the conclusion that Carlisle's gift is super-compassion, understood as the superhuman ability to form caring relationships with everyone, even strangers, and that is what enables him to live in the world in a way that no other vampire can.

NOTES

1. Stephenie Meyer, *Twilight* (New York: Little, Brown and Company, 2005), p. 307.

2. Ibid., p. 248.

3. *Midnight Sun* (partial draft) is the name of a manuscript that Stephenie Meyer began that explored the events of the original *Twilight* novel from the perspective of Edward (which included a number of scenes with the Cullens not found in the original novel). Unfortunately, some lowlife took an unfinished draft and posted it illegally (without the author's permission) on the Internet. As a result, Meyer has abandoned work on the novel that would have been *Midnight Sun* due to this violation of her trust and rights. And so, we may never see things from Edward's perspective. Meyer, after announcing

her decision, made a partial draft of the manuscript available on her Web site (www .stepheniemeyer.com/pdf/midnightsun_partial_draft4.pdf). In referencing this work, we acknowledge Meyer's own statement that this was always a work in progress that she has been forced to make public by someone else's inexcusable behavior. So, while this cannot be considered the official version of events, we take this draft in the spirit that Meyer offered it to her fans, as stated on her Web site: "I hope this fragment gives you further insight into Edward's head and adds a new dimension to the Twilight story."

4. *Midnight Sun* (partial draft), pp. 69–70.

5. Bryan Van Norden, *Mengzi: With Selections from Traditional Commentaries* (Indianapolis, IN: Hackett Publishing, 2008), p. 46.

6. The Dalai Lama, *The Compassionate Life* (Boston: Wisdom Publications, 2001), p. 21.

7. Michael Slote, *The Ethics of Care and Empathy* (New York: Routledge, 2007), p. 27.

8. Nel Noddings, *Caring: A Feminine Approach to Ethics and Moral Education* (Berkeley: University of California Press, 1984), p. 86.

9. Stephenie Meyer, *Breaking Dawn* (New York: Little, Brown and Company, 2008), p. 717.

10. Ibid., pp. 718–719.

11. *Midnight Sun* (partial draft), p. 215.

PART TWO

NEW MOON

VAMPIRE-DÄMMERUNG: WHAT CAN *TWILIGHT* TELL US ABOUT GOD?

Peter S. Fosl and Eli Fosl

Vampires are typically creatures of moral darkness who turn good people into bloodthirsty, cold-blooded killers like themselves.[1] Consider the Count in the 1931 film *Dracula*, played by Béla Lugosi (Bella Swan's namesake); such vampires seem particularly fond of mesmerizing innocent young women before feeding upon them.[2] Bloodsuckers are often portrayed as fearsome beings associated with dark, satanic forces, like the ghoul in F. W. Murnau's *Nosferatu* (1922) or the fiends of John Carpenter's *Vampires* (1998).

In fact, the very existence of vampires raises an ancient philosophical question: Why would God—who is supposed to be all-good, all-powerful, and all-knowing—allow the existence of such despicable creatures? Certainly, God could annihilate every vampire in existence. Or God could have prevented vampires from coming into existence in the first place by neutralizing the magic, or spiritual power, or infection, or venom, or mutation, or whatever it is upon which their existence depends. But for some reason God—if there is a God—does not rid the world of evil and, at least in fiction, of vampires.

Why, more generally, God does not (or cannot) eliminate evil from the world has long been a topic of sharp debate among philosophers. Technically, philosophers have, since the eighteenth century, called this issue the problem of "theodicy." Those philosophers who wish to defend God against charges of negligence, impotence, or nonexistence have produced a variety of answers to the questions theodicy poses. Unfortunately, as we'll see in our discussion of *Twilight*, these answers are unsatisfactory. But thankfully *Twilight* advances a distinctive answer of its own.

The very name "twilight" suggests a place of ambiguity—a place that's neither fully dark nor fully light. Twilight can refer both to dawn and dusk, both to a time when things are getting lighter and when they are getting darker. The nineteenth-century German philosopher Friedrich Nietzsche (1844–1900) played on just this ambiguity in his book *Götzen-Dämmerung*, translated as *Twilight of the Idols* (1889), a title that we like to imagine Stephenie Meyer herself plays on.[3] The ambiguity of twilight points to a response—if not a proper solution—that the *Twilight* narrative poses to the problem of theodicy. *Twilight*'s solution might briefly be described in this way: Good and evil are ambiguous terms, not as fixed or as clear as convention portrays. Good can become evil, and evil, good; it's largely within the power of both humans and vampires to determine the moral compasses of their own lives. The story positions human beings and vampires as good in acts of self-overcoming, overcoming their nature, their social standing, and the traditional ways good and evil are configured (at least with regard to vampires). It's up to young people like Bella and Edward

Cullen to determine whether they are in the dawn or dusk of their lives. In other words, dawn does not break, it must be broken.

What does this say about God? Not much that's terribly favorable. If God or a god does exist in the world of *Twilight*, it must be a deity who either is not all-powerful (and therefore cannot prevent the evil of the world) or has abandoned the world, leaving people to fend for themselves. The good news of *Twilight* is that, at least in the case of Bella and Edward, young people are up to the task.

Let's turn now to consider some of the answers philosophers have advanced to the problem of theodicy, and see how *Twilight* fits their models.

Evil's Not a Problem, Because Evil Doesn't Exist

Mary Baker Eddy (1821–1910), the founder of the Christian Science movement, maintained that evil is, in a fundamental way, not real. As she said, "Evil is a negation, because it is the absence of truth. It is nothing, because it is the absence of something. It is unreal, because it presupposes the absence of God, the omnipotent and omnipresent. Every mortal must learn that there is neither power nor reality in evil."[4] Plato (428–348 BCE), Plotinus (204–270), Augustine (354–450), Benedict Spinoza (1632–1677), and G. W. Leibniz (1646–1716) each presented variations of this theme in their philosophical works.[5] Augustine, for example, who was deeply influenced by the Platonists, wrote in chapter 11 of his *Enchiridion*:

> For the almighty God, who, as even the heathen acknowledge, has supreme power over all things, being Himself supremely good, would never permit the existence of anything evil among His works, if He were

not so omnipotent and good that He can bring good even out of evil. For what is that which we call evil but the absence of good? In the bodies of animals, disease and wounds mean nothing but the absence of health; for when a cure is effected, that does not mean that the evils which were present—namely, the diseases and wounds—go away from the body and dwell elsewhere: they altogether cease to exist; for the wound or disease is not a substance but a defect in the fleshly substance— the flesh itself being a substance, and therefore something good, of which those evils—that is, privations of the good which we call health—are accidents. Just in the same way, what are called vices in the soul are nothing but privations of natural good. And when they are not transferred elsewhere: when they cease to exist in the healthy soul, they cannot exist anywhere else.[6]

A corollary to this point has been picked up by various philosophers: In the case of immoral human conduct, evil indicates a lack of *human* being. Those who behave immorally are those who have become degraded humans, less than fully human. As people like to say, those who are evil act like animals.

In *Twilight*, then, we should ask whether the vampires, or really anyone who is configured as evil, is depicted as subhuman or like a nonhuman animal. Vampires bite people, drink blood, and possess astounding physical abilities, and in other vampire stories even turn into bats. Certainly, none of the vampires in *Twilight* seems close to God; and both James and Victoria, the villains of *Twilight* and *Eclipse*, might be interpreted to be degraded humans.[7] So at first blush it's easy to conclude that the *Twilight* series conforms to this philosophical tradition, depicting evil in animal-like, nonhuman ways.

But then, on the other hand, the Cullens' coven hardly seems evil, even though they are in certain ways animal-like.

And of course, we need to consider the Quileutes. The Quileute wolves are definitely related to nonhumans; they run through the forest and devour raw flesh. But they're not depicted as evil—quite the contrary. The example of Jacob Black's people, then, as well as the virtuous Cullens, dashes the evil-as-privation-of-being model, and it doesn't explain how things work in *Twilight*. Therefore, let us continue.

Evil's Not a Problem, Because Evil Indicates Ignorance

Another, similar view is that evil or belief in evil is a matter of ignorance. By this account, one who is not fully human cannot fully know what it is to be good. So for Socrates and Plato, at least, no one does evil knowingly, and all apparently evil acts are mistakes about what's good. When, conversely, people come to know (really *know*) the truth about the world, about the divine, and about goodness, they just don't behave badly anymore. That sort of ignorance affects people's self-knowledge. Consequently, people who don't really know goodness do not and *cannot* truly know themselves. So does this sort of account of goodness and evil make sense of the world depicted in *Twilight*?

Again, at first it does seem plausible that in *Twilight* the good are knowledgeable while the evil are ignorant. The four louts who accost Bella in Port Angeles (literally, the doorway of angels) in the first volume, *Twilight*, might easily be thought of as ignorant.[8] And Carlisle Cullen (not to mention Edward) is repeatedly shown to be a man of great knowledge and taste. Carlisle is cultured, he is a doctor (which in Latin literally means "learned"), and by all accounts he is good. Moreover, the apple on the cover of *Twilight* calls forth not only the forbidden temptations of the Garden of Eden but the path to sin and evil.[9]

Even though metaphorically Bella bites the apple, the story hardly portrays her as bad for doing so. And do we really have any reason to think of James or Victoria as ignorant? Similarly, Bella's mother and father, along with nearly every other good human being, remain profoundly ignorant of some very important dimensions of the world. So in *Twilight* it's neither the case that the good are consistently knowledgeable nor the case that the evil are consistently ignorant.

Conceiving of evil as an illusion or as born of ignorance doesn't work very well. As it is in *Twilight*, so it often is in our world: The good are ignorant and the evil are in the know (and vice versa). Moreover, so far as God is concerned, these theories don't really resolve the question of theodicy. They just change the question from why God permits evil to why God permits privation, ignorance, and error. Couldn't God make moral truths perfectly plain, clear, distinct, and indubitable to everyone? Couldn't God have made it so that nothing exists in a degenerate or privative way? There seems no reason to think otherwise. So let's try another theory.

Evil's Not a Problem, Because It's the Necessary Cost of Good

A more promising cluster of philosophical theories attempting to explain why God doesn't eliminate evil argue that evil is somehow *necessary for goodness*—that goodness can exist, at least for humans, only if evil also exists. One way of comprehending this strategy is to think about the problem of evil in logical terms. Just as up implies down, the very idea of "goodness," one might say, requires "evil" as a contrasting term—especially if one wants to understand and appreciate what goodness really means. Along related lines, Augustine wrote, "And in the universe, even that which is called evil, when it is regulated and put in its own place, only enhances our admiration of the good; for we enjoy and value the good more when we compare it with the evil."[10]

Unfortunately, this strategy won't work, either. For one thing, if the issue just concerns what it takes to *know* or *admire* goodness, couldn't God simply insert that knowledge or admiration into our minds? More radically, if the existence of evil is the price of knowing goodness, wouldn't it be better for humans never to acquire that knowledge, to remain in the same ignorant bliss that characterized Adam and Eve before they bit the fruit of moral knowledge? If moral knowledge requires vampires or Edward committing suicide (as he tries to do in *New Moon*), then we think it better to give up that knowledge along with the vampires, and not let Edward or anyone else kill himself.[11]

Wouldn't it be possible for everyone to understand what evil is without anyone actually doing evil things? Couldn't everyone know what the phrase "living below the equator" means without anyone actually living below the equator? And here's another alternative: Why not replace the contrasting terms of "good" and "evil" with the terms "good" and "better" or even "good" and "good in a different way"? A world of (a) different goods or (b) different degrees of goodness seems just as knowable and just as possible as a world of (c) good and evil.

But there is a deeper strength to the claim that goodness requires evil that we need to face, since there do seem to be particular goods that require at least the possibility of evil. How could Bella have demonstrated courage and a willingness to sacrifice herself for her mother if James's evil weren't part of her world? How could Edward and the Cullens exhibit the virtues of loyalty in the face of the Volturi if the Volturi's menacing power hadn't really been demonstrated? Could Edward really have been so good if he weren't tempted by the dark desire to devour Bella? Could Edward and Bella's relationship become so deep and passionate if the world they inhabit weren't shot through with danger, peril, and beings of malign intent?

The necessity of evil for certain goods is one dimension of what Leibniz meant when he advanced the seemingly silly idea that ours is the best of all possible worlds. One way of interpreting Leibniz's claim is along the lines laid out in the first section of this chapter—that evil must only be apparent. If only we could see how apparent evil fits into and makes possible a maximally good whole, we would accept it as it is. Leibniz wrote:

> The infinite wisdom of the Almighty allied with his boundless goodness has brought it about that nothing better could have been created. As a consequence all things are in perfect harmony and conspire in the most beautiful way. . . . Whenever, therefore, some detail of the world of God appears to us reprehensible, we should judge that we do not know enough about it and that according to the wise who would understand it, nothing better could even be desired.[12]

Of course, the evils of the world are certainly real enough and well-known enough to those who suffer them. That's perhaps the principal reason Leibniz's claim seems silly to so many.[13] But if one argues the alternative we're considering here, perhaps the idea actually makes sense. From a God's-eye point of view, according to this account, considering the creation as a whole, it is a better balance to have a world with both goods, and the evils those goods require, than to have no world at all.

Defenders of God's goodness cite free will as the principal good that requires evil. Free will is heralded by God's defenders to be such an important capacity that it's worth accepting all of the evil it often makes possible. And, of course, free will gets God off the hook, since it's people who exercise their freedom badly who are to blame for evil. Indeed, the *Twilight* series is structured in a way consistent with this idea.

Living in a town called Forks, which symbolizes the many forks in the road of life Bella encounters, Bella's story is very much one of choices. Should she choose to pursue a relationship with a vampire? Should she become a vampire? Should she choose Jacob or Edward? Should she give birth to Renesmee? An odyssey like hers would be impossible, or would at least be farcical, if her choices were determined by inexorable forces beyond her control. But more important for our purposes here, free choice like Bella's would seem to be senseless if the range of choices didn't include evil choices—the sort of choices Victoria and James make.

But would free choice really be impossible without evil outcomes? For one thing, free choice might be exercised among a range of various goods (like choosing between Jacob and Edward) rather than goods and evils. Why not construct a world where there are lots of goods to choose from, but no evils? Free choice doesn't require an unlimited range of choices. One can find going to an ice cream shop and choosing among many good flavors extremely satisfying, even without the possibility that one of them might be poison.

We are not really sure that people either in the real world or in *Twilight* have unlimited free will regardless. Is Bella really so free that she could decide to kill Edward or Renesmee? Could you really choose to kill an innocent child for no reason? And would it really be so awful if every choice were determined, say, by chemical processes of nervous systems? People would still experience everything they do now—including the feeling that they're making their own choices.

But as Russian philosopher-novelist Fyodor Dostoevsky (1821–1881) argued in *The Brothers Karamazov* (1880), it's not morally defensible to justify one's own good on the basis of the suffering of others. Similarly, one can't defensibly hold that the existence of murdering, bloodsucking vampires is a good thing because it makes possible an intense romantic relationship between two teenagers. Moreover, comparing the evil endured by individuals to the "goodness" of the whole trivializes individuals. It's possible that from what Spinoza called the "view from eternity," the whole looks "good." But from the perspective of the individual who suffers evil (a perspective that must count if individuals are to be respected as beings of moral worth) God's eye is irrelevant—and actually, not even all that good.[14]

Evil, Transcendence, and Natural Goodness

If the divine appears anywhere in the *Twilight* series, it's in Jacob's world, the world of the Quileute Native Americans. Meyer gives an account of the origins of Quileute wolves in *New Moon* that roots them in a supernatural, magical connection between Jacob's tribe and its "spirit warriors."[15] But she gives readers no corresponding account of the origins of vampires, supernatural or otherwise.

Indeed, one of the most striking things about the *Twilight* series is the way it strips vampirism of its usual supernatural character.[16] Vampires are normally portrayed as perversions of traditional ideas of the Christian sacred. Bram Stoker's *Dracula* (1897) as well as Francis Ford Coppola's *Dracula* (1992), for example, depict vampires engaged in inversions of many Christian sacraments—an inverted marriage, an inverted burial, and so on. Instead of gaining immortality through the blood of Christ, vampires gain it through the blood of people. Vampires, like the Christ, offer eternal life, but they do so only in the form of eternal living death. Vampires flee crucifixes and are burned by holy water. But in *Twilight* the roots of vampirism seem lost in the mists of time.[17] They seem to have no relation to Christianity or religion at all—at least, not with the new generation of vampires.

The Volturi, on the other hand, are from Italy, and that in itself connects them to the Catholic Church—a representative of old-school ideas about God, good, and evil. The Volturi are also aristocratic (an old-school social-political order) and prey on humans (the traditional way of life among vampires). As they enforce traditional vampire law, it makes sense to see the Volturi as representatives of tradition. But the Cullens are deviants from (and even rebels against) the old codes. Traditional relationships of the good to the evil, the human to the vampire, and God to the world, don't apply to them. They have spurned religion, both light and dark.

In *New Moon* the Cullens clash with the Volturi on the basis of Bella's and Edward's choices, and the fruit of those choices, because they no longer adhere to the old code. Bella, Edward, and the Cullens prevail, suggesting that the heroes of this story have transcended the traditions, the customs, and the idea of a Christian God. They live through the darkness of a new moon (the opposite of a fully lighted full moon) and enter a new *Breaking Dawn* of their own creation, not the creation of God or nature. In this, the *Twilight* series presents a view much like that of the French philosopher Jean-Paul Sartre's (1905–1980) existentialism, a philosophy describing and advocating people living lives of self-transcendence grounded neither in God nor in nature but only in their own free choices.[18]

Bella's choice of Edward over Jacob indicates her choice of a path to happiness different from that offered by tradition, God, and nature. In fact, both Edward and Bella achieve a life of goodness and happiness through what might be called self-transcendence. They go beyond the natural order.

God is often associated with the natural order as presupposed creator of that order. So by the traditional account, to become good is to act in accordance with one's nature and to perfect one's nature (and in doing so, conform to God's design). But what makes Edward and the Cullens good is that they deny their nature as vampires.[19] Their goodness is defined by the restraint of their desires (as Stoic philosophers of every age have recommended), with not killing and not feeding on humans.[20] Moreover, the goodness of the Cullens is defined not only by their refusing to do bad to humans; it is also signified by their actually doing humans good. Consider, for example, Carlisle's choice to heal humans as a doctor.[21] Both in restraining their desires and in doing good rather than bad to humans, the Cullens have transcended their vampire nature, traditionally conceived.

Like Edward, Bella follows a path of self-transcendence. She makes choices that change her from girl to woman to mother. She intentionally sets in motion events that transform her from human being to vampire. She changes from weak to strong, from pawn to queen (the most powerful piece on the chessboard used on the cover of *Breaking Dawn*). Even the symbolism of events in Bella's and Edward's relationship points to self-transcendence as well as their transcendence of nature and nature's God. In choosing Edward over Jacob, for example, Bella chooses to bite the apple that will carry her away from the Eden-like natural-magical world of Jacob into a different world with Edward—from a traditional point of view, a fallen world where she will have to face death and suffering.

In another symbolic series of events, when Bella leaves the world of her town and first visits Edward's home in *Twilight*, he carries her upward—as if she is riding Phaedrus's chariot,[22] out of the misty, obscure, old world in which she had lived to the top of a Nietzschean mountain (a place of self-overcoming),[23] to the top of a majestic tree (a phallic symbol), to a place where her vision of the world is expanded and where she can see things in a new light. In that new light not only Edward's skin, but her world as a whole, is transformed. And what she had previously considered to be good and evil is transformed along with it. What would have been thought of as ugly and evil (vampires) in Bella's former world now glitters with beauty and goodness. What had before been thought of as threatening is now protective. But the new light in which things are seen is not divine light, and in a metaphorical way not even natural light. The light through which Bella's world is transformed is the light of her and Edward's choices—choices that carry them beyond their natures and beyond the terms of the worlds they had formerly inhabited.[24]

So what does this imply about God? If God or a God-like being exists in the world of *Twilight*, we can conclude either that it *cannot* prevent evil or, for no good reason, that it *will not* prevent evil. As we've seen, the defenses of the traditional conception of God just don't work. It may be that God's powers are restricted to the act of creation and do not include the power to intervene in the world. It may be that God has abandoned the world. Or, of course, perhaps there just is no God. So far as the humans and vampires of *Twilight* are concerned, however, this isn't necessarily a bad thing. God, even if the creator of the natural order, is not the only source of happiness, or even of goodness, in *Twilight*. Both Bella and Edward refuse religion and transcend both their own natures and nature's God. They find happiness and goodness not through God's salvation, not through miraculous intervention, and not through the natural way of things, but rather, by relying on only their decidedly unnatural selves. *Twilight*'s answer to the question of theodicy is, then, that whether or not God exists, we are free of God and able to find happiness, power, and immortality on our own.

NOTES

1. There are, of course, notable exceptions outside the *Twilight* universe, including Joss Whedon's *Angel*, Bill from *True Blood*, and Louis from Anne Rice's *Vampire Chronicles*.

2. Bella Swan is the heroine of the *Twilight* series. Besides the association her name draws with horror movie star Béla Lugosi, the name more literally means "beautiful" as, for example, in the phrase a "southern belle." We suppose one might also say

that the name suggests that Bella is someone who resonates when struck by the blows of life.

3. Nietzsche's book *Götzen-Dämmerung* played off the title Richard Wagner gave to the last part of *The Ring*, his great opera. Wagner called that part *Twilight of the Gods* (*Götterdämmerung*, 1876).

4. Mary Baker Eddy, *Science and Health* (Boston: Joseph Armstrong, 1906), p. 186.

5. In Spinoza's 1665 letter to Blyenbergh, he wrote, "For my own part, I cannot admit that sin and evil have any positive existence, far less that anything can exist, or come to pass, contrary to the will of G-D. On the contrary, not only do I assert that sin has no positive existence, I also maintain that only in speaking improperly, or humanly, can we say that we sin against G-D, as in the expression that men offend G-D." A translation by Terry Neff can be found at http://home.earthlink.net/~tneff/build3.htm#TOP?/~tneff/letters.htm.

6. Augustine, *Enchiridion*, trans. by M. Dods, chap. 10–11, in *The Essential Augustine*, ed. V. J. Bourke (Indianapolis: Hackett Publishing, 1974), p. 65.

7. Stephenie Meyer, *Twilight* (New York: Little, Brown and Company, 2005); Stephenie Meyer, *Eclipse* (New York: Little, Brown and Company, 2007).

8. *Twilight*, p. 157.

9. There was, of course, a second tree in the Garden of Eden, a tree of life. Could the apple on the cover also (or instead) refer to the vampire's promise of eternal life?

10. Augustine, *Enchiridion*, p. 65.

11. Stephenie Meyer, *New Moon* (New York: Little, Brown and Company, 2006), p. 419.

12. G. W. Leibniz, *Monadology and Other Philosophical Essays*, trans. by P. Schrecker and A. M. Schrecker (Indianapolis: Bobbs-Merrill, 1965), pp. 123–124.

13. Voltaire mocked in his book *Candide* (1759) Leibniz's characterization of this as the best of all possible worlds.

14. Benedict Spinoza, *Ethics* (Part 2, Proposition 44, Corollary 2); "*sub quadam specie aeternitatis*" ("under the aspect of eternity," describing universal truth without depending on temporal aspects of reality).

15. *New Moon*, p. 245 ff.

16. A strategy also taken by the recent horror film *30 Days of Night* (2007), drawn from Steve Niles and Ben Templesmith's comic book series (2002).

17. Curiously, other recent vampire stories also elide the religious dimension of vampirism. Vampires and werewolves of the *Underworld* saga (2003, 2006, 2009) are also romanticized, and like the Daywalker in *Blade* (1998) their existence is explained as a result of natural biology. *Twilight*'s vampires, however, aren't depicted as produced by biological disease or mutation, and their refusal to procreate biologically looks decidedly unnatural.

18. Jean-Paul Sartre, *Being and Nothingness* (New York: Washington Square Press, 1993).

19. Along these lines, the story of Bella and Edward's romance has been interpreted as a morality tale about sexual abstinence and restraint. But we'd like to argue that

Twilight is not only about self-denial and self-restraint or even altruism; it's also and more deeply about self-transformation.

20. The Cullens are not Stoics, however, in the sense that for Stoics, repressing desire actually meant conforming to nature.

21. The Daywalker in the *Blade* films (1998, 2002, 2004), for example, is defined as good because he not only keeps in check his desire to feed off of humans but also because he undertakes the risky project of helping them. The films, of course, are based on Marv Wolfman's and Gene Colan's 1973 comic.

22. In his dialogue *Phaedrus*, Plato described a chariot that can carry one to the hyper-uranian heavens and see reality in a different, superior way. It is a chariot, however, that requires the strength of a "dark" horse to make its ascent.

23. In *Thus Spake Zarathustra* (1885), Nietzsche described how philosophers who have achieved self-overcoming inhabit the mountaintops of philosophical understanding, separated from ordinary culture, seeing the world in a clearer, more complete way.

24. The *Twilight* saga has often been criticized as sexist. It describes the journey of, yes, a strong-willed young woman who gets what she wants. But, critics point out, it's the story of a young woman whose agency boils down to manipulating a man to act upon her, to inject something into her, to make her more like him, and to give her a child. She achieves happiness not by becoming a distinctively new kind of woman but by affirming—contrary to so much else in the series—the aspirations of traditional womanhood. It's a fairly persuasive criticism in our view—so far as it goes. But we'd like to point out that there's something more to Bella's story. Her story, like Edward's, despite its flaws, is a tale of a new generation that critically turns its back on the old ways and realizes the possibilities of self-transcendence by establishing new values through the power of their own choices.

TO BITE OR NOT TO BITE: *TWILIGHT*, IMMORTALITY, AND THE MEANING OF LIFE

Brendan Shea

I can't always be Lois Lane. I want to be Superman, too.

—Bella Swan, *Twilight*[1]

Over the course of the *Twilight* series, Bella Swan gradually succeeds at convincing Edward Cullen to turn her into a vampire. When Edward questions her about *why* she wants to become a vampire, she repeatedly says that it is out of love for him. On one level, she might hope that by becoming a vampire she could better understand Edward's emotions and abilities and could thereby love him more fully. On another level, however, Bella's desire is for *immortality*, and her underlying worry is that her human mortality is in conflict with the goals she has in life. As Bella understands it, much of her life's purpose is provided by the love she feels for Edward, Jacob Black, and her extended "family." Insofar as her eventual death will prevent her from being there to protect and guide the people she loves, Bella might think that choosing immortality is the best thing for her to do.

But is Bella correct in thinking that there is a conflict between love and mortality? Or is there something about love, and about living a meaningful human life, that actually *requires* her mortality? These questions, while hypothetical, are of real philosophical interest. After all, Bella's love for others, her reason for living, will strike many of us as resembling our own reasons for living. If she's right in choosing to become a vampire, this suggests that our mortality is in conflict with the goals of love, and that this is our misfortune. If she's wrong, it would suggest there's something valuable in our mortality. The questions that confront Bella are specific versions of those that confront us all: What constitutes a meaningful human life? What choices should we make in order to live such a life?

More Love and Death

> Though it seems to men that they live by care for
> themselves, in truth it is love alone by which they live.
>
> —Leo Tolstoy[2]

Bella first seriously considers becoming a vampire toward the end of *Twilight*. James attacks and bites Bella, but Edward prevents Bella from becoming a vampire by sucking the venom out of her wound. When Bella wakes up in the hospital, she criticizes Edward's action and argues that it would have been better to allow her to become a vampire. Bella worries that her mortality will prevent her from truly loving Edward. Her concerns are, in fact, expressions of a classic philosophical question: Is it possible to live a meaningful life if one must eventually cease to exist?

While Bella is in the hospital, she worries that "I may not die now . . . but I'm going to die sometime. Every minute of the day, I get closer. And I'm going to get *old*."[3] Later, after the prom, she tells Edward that "mostly, I dream about being with you forever."[4] Bella's love for Edward is expressed in terms of certain *desires*. She wants to spend time with Edward, to be physically intimate with him, to protect him from harm, and to help him pursue the things he values. These desires show up in Bella's choice of Edward over Jacob, and in her willingness to take risks on Edward's behalf.

Bella believes that love (in particular for Edward) makes her life meaningful—it gives her goals to pursue. Mortality, unfortunately, seems to *guarantee* that Bella cannot fulfill these goals. As a human, she will one day die, and when she does, everyone she loves will be left to struggle on without her. Thus, mortality might seem to doom Bella to a meaningless existence—to a life with a purpose she can never achieve.

Leo Tolstoy (1828–1910), in his autobiographical book *My Confession*, recounted his own attempts to reconcile the knowledge of his mortality with his desire to live a meaningful life. Like Bella, Tolstoy worried that if we must die, and if there is no afterlife, then all of our lives are necessarily meaningless. He claimed that our situation is analogous to that of a traveler clinging to a twig halfway down the side of a deep well. There is a beast waiting to eat him at the top of the well and a dragon at the bottom. His death is assured by two mice that are gnawing on the branch. Tolstoy went on:

> But while he is still hanging there he sees some drops of honey on the leaves of the bush, stretches out his tongue and licks them. In the same way I am clinging

to the tree of life, knowing full well the dragon of death inevitably awaits me, ready to tear me to pieces, and I cannot understand how I have fallen into this torment. And I try licking the honey that once consoled me, but it no longer gives me pleasure. The white mouse and the black mouse—day and night—are gnawing at the branch from which I am hanging. I see the dragon clearly and the honey no longer tastes sweet . . . and this is no fable but the truth, the truth that is irrefutable and intelligible to everyone.[5]

The problem, for both Bella and Tolstoy, seems to be that the knowledge that we will one day die prevents us from enjoying the pleasures—the honey—that life has to offer.

Tolstoy considered and rejected several potential solutions to this problem. First, we might ignore the knowledge that we must die, and live as if this were not the case. Tolstoy claimed this is impossible, and Bella's experience provides some support for his view. Second, we might live for our family and friends. But Tolstoy thought this also must ultimately fail—after all, they will die as well, and so any good we can achieve for them is at best temporary. Finally, we might live for the moment, and enjoy the good things with the knowledge that they will one day be gone. To Tolstoy, and to Bella, this seems a bit hollow, insofar as it involves accepting that nothing one does will ever "really" matter. Tolstoy concluded that life can only be meaningful if the soul is in some sense immortal.

But there are a few reasons for thinking that Bella and Tolstoy might be mistaken. First, their view assumes that any worthwhile life must change the world in some permanent way. Bella's actions, however, suggest that she can't really believe this. She risks her life repeatedly to save her mother, to save Edward, and to save her child. These sacrifices presumably would be worthwhile even if she knew that all the people she risked herself for must *eventually* die. Imagine that the Volturi manage to kill Bella, the werewolves, and the Cullens at the end of the fourth book; more than this, imagine that Alice Cullen tells Bella ahead of time that this will happen. While this certainly would have been tragic, it seems unlikely that Bella would suddenly stop thinking it worthwhile to help her loved ones. So perhaps there's hope for a meaningful mortal life after all.

Even if Bella and Tolstoy are correct in their supposition that a meaningful life must leave a permanent mark, there is no reason to think that a mortal person couldn't lead such a life. Mortals can leave permanent marks on the universe in all sorts of ways. They can have children, write books that inspire others, or pursue careers that help others. They can fight for just causes, as the Cullens do against the Volturi, and try to leave the world a better place for those who come after them. Just as being mortal doesn't prevent us from making a positive difference, being immortal doesn't guarantee that we will make one. If you spend your immortal life eating humans (as most vampires do), this would certainly not leave the world better off.

Bella has a motivation for becoming immortal that most of us don't have, of course: Edward is already a powerful and elegant immortal, while she is a clumsy mortal. Even if she recognizes the possibility of *other* people living meaningful mortal lives, she might think that she can't do so. Her love requires that she be able to help *Edward* in some meaningful way. So, she says, "I'll be the first to admit that I have no experience with relationships. But it just seems logical . . . a man and woman have to be somewhat equal . . . as in, one of them can't always be swooping in and saving the other one. They have to save each other *equally*."[6] As a mere mortal, Bella will be unable to do anything for Edward he cannot do for himself. Moreover, her life span will be only a fraction of his, and thus she risks becoming a mere footnote in the story of his life. Edward recognizes this worry, but initially refuses her request nevertheless. He worries, of course, that Bella will lose her soul in the process.

On Losing One's Soul

Therefore death is nothing to us, nothing\That matters at all, since mind we know is mortal.

—Lucretius[7]

If Bella's worry is that she can't properly love Edward as a mortal, his worry is the opposite. He worries that he has already lost his soul, and that making Bella a vampire will strip her of her soul as well. He tells Bella that "I cannot be without you, but I will not destroy your soul,"[8] and later pines, "If there were any way for me to become human for you—no matter what the price was, I would pay it."[9] Carlisle Cullen explains Edward's fear as a fear that God won't accept him, or that there can be no afterlife for him. But there's another worry too. Both Edward and Rosalie Cullen seem at times to regret their immortality, feeling that they've lost something valuable. Just as Bella's worry about death should strike us as plausible, so should this latter pair's ambiguous attitude toward immortality. If our souls are the things (whatever they are) that make us human, the question becomes: Could a vampire have one?

Imagine for a moment that you are Carlisle. It's morning; you spent the sleepless night listening to music and rereading your favorite book for the thirtieth time. You go downstairs and say good-bye to your family. You're never tired, so there's no point to picking up coffee on the way to work. You only need to hunt for your food once a month or so, so there's no such thing as a family breakfast. It's cold outside, but you don't notice. You'll never get ill from underdressing, or not washing your hands, or eating the wrong thing; you'll never be out of shape or be tired after a long day's work. There's no need to give your children a ride to school, or to worry when they are not home on time. The last time one was hit by a car, the vehicle was the victim. You go to the hospital where you've worked for the last several years. Some of your colleagues worry that they've wasted the prime of lives and that they never can get back the long hours they've dedicated to the hospital. Their children have grown up and moved away. Yours, of course, will remain exactly as they've always been.

Outside of the occasional disagreements with rival vampire clans, there is no real danger in the Cullens' lives. This may sound quite pleasant until we consider how *inhuman* such a life would be. In particular, it's hard to see how such a life could have the same type of meaning or purpose that a well-structured human life does. Bella's love and sacrifice for others gives meaning to her life. Edward's love for Bella can never quite be the same. His choice to stay in Forks, unlike Bella's, does not involve any real sacrifice. Bella's mother will get older, and her Phoenix friends will move away to college. Edward's family remains unchanged, and he always has an infinite amount of time to travel and go to college. Likewise, Edward's risks on Bella's behalf are at first relatively trivial. Edward risks nothing when he saves Bella from being hit by a car, or when he scares away the thugs in Port Angeles. For ordinary humans, these acts would be incredible expressions of love; for Edward, they are no more than we ought to expect.

Contemporary philosopher Martha Nussbaum has argued that the relationships and goals that give human lives meaning and value *require* that these lives have a permanent end. In an article about the philosopher Lucretius (96–55 BCE), she argues that "for many, if not all, of the elements of human life that we consider the most valuable, the value they have cannot be fully explained without mentioning the circumstances of finite and mortal existence."[10] Nussbaum specifically argues that immortals could not be courageous insofar as courage "consists in a certain way of acting and reacting in the face of death and the danger of death."[11] This same invulnerability also undercuts the ability of immortals to be genuine lovers or friends. To be a genuine lover or friend is to be prepared to make sacrifices, but immortals simply have no way to sacrifice themselves.

Nussbaum suggests that, on reflection, one can see that nearly every human value is incompatible with immortality. As the Volturi government shows, there is little need for social *justice* among vampires, in the sense of creating a society that helps the worst off. *Thrift*, as demonstrated by the Cullens' enormous wealth, is meaningless to those who have an infinite amount of time to gather money. The same point holds for virtues such as moderation or dedication to a craft. For a person like Edward, who wants to dedicate his life to loving Bella, immortality might thus be a curse rather than a blessing.

Twilight's vampires are not Greek gods, of course, and the Cullens are capable of being killed. The Volturi, in particular, introduce an element of real danger that allows for the Cullens to demonstrate the human virtues of courage, love, and loyalty. But Nussbaum's argument need not entail an absolute distinction between those who are capable of love or courage, and those who aren't. Instead, we should recognize that love and courage come in various degrees, and that the capacity to realize these virtues is linked to one's invulnerability to death or pain. On this view, it is simply more *difficult* for creatures like vampires to be loving or courageous, though it might not be impossible.

The world described in the *Twilight* books supports Nussbaum's claim. The vampires are to a large extent as Nussbaum describes the Greek gods—they pursue their own pleasure, have few close friends, and value preserving their own lives above everything else. They, like other immortals described in literature, simply have no reason to value things like friendship, justice, or courage. In the absence of such human values, they devote their lives to the pursuit of more immediate bodily pleasures. Nussbaum's general point is also supported by *Twilight*'s stories of old werewolves, who *chose* to age and die normally once the vampiric threat receded.

The Cullens, and in particular Carlisle, provide a partial answer to Edward's and Nussbaum's worries about immortality. Carlisle, unlike many of the other vampires, does not seem to need the threat of danger to motivate him to acts of love or compassion. In fact, his life seems to be the paradigm of meaningful life. He spends his days working at a hospital and his nights with his family. He has saved many of his family members from premature death and still serves as something like a "father" to his immortal "children." The attraction of Carlisle's "alternative" lifestyle is clearly recognized by others of his kind—Alice seeks him out, and both Jasper and Emmet seem to take him as a role model. While the actions of the amoral Volturi feed Edward's fear that he has no soul, Carlisle represents the possibility of living a meaningful immortal existence.

The possibility of Carlisle living this meaningful life requires that *other* people be mortal, however. Carlisle's work in a hospital, for example, only makes sense if there are creatures capable of sickness and death. If everyone in the world were a vampire, there would certainly be far less need for such work. Even Carlisle's role as father depends on his saving the children from sure death and helping them to adjust to their new life. If *everyone* were guaranteed immortality, there would simply be no one Carlisle could help. This does not show, of course, that immortals must live *meaningless* lives. Instead, they must find new values to give structure to their lives. And these new values may be quite different from the type one might expect.

I'm Bored . . .

I guess things are going to be kind of boring now, aren't they?

—Jacob Black, *Breaking Dawn*[12]

At the close of *Breaking Dawn*, Bella and her allies appear to be well on their way to "happily ever after." One could imagine how the years after the close of the book might go. Renesmee grows quickly to adulthood and moves away with Jacob. Charlie and Renee grow old and die; alternatively, they become vampires and move in with the rest of the clan. Bella travels the world, attends a variety of famous colleges, and writes a novel of her own. But what then? What will Bella and Edward do two hundred years from now? Or two thousand years from now? Eventually, they will have seen every sight and read every book. If they devote themselves to the task, they may succeed in ridding the world of the Volturi, or even in converting all vampires to their brand of "vegetarianism." There will, at some point, be nothing left to interest them. After thousands of years, they may even lose any need or desire to speak to each other—each knows what the other will say, and without the person saying it. The problem, it seems, is one of *boredom*.

The philosopher Bernard Williams (1929–2003) considered the problem of boredom by analyzing a character named Elina Makropulos, who appears in a play by Karel Capek (1890–1938). Three hundred years before the play's action begins, Elina drank a potion that gave her immortality. This has not worked out well for her, however, since her unending life "has come to a state of boredom, indifference, and coldness. Everything is joyless."[13] Williams argued that this is a necessary consequence of Elina's immortality, since there is no way a meaningful *human* life could go on forever. According to Williams, our lives are directed at the fulfillment of certain *categorical desires*—desires whose fulfillment is not conditioned on our being around to see them fulfilled. Hunger and lust, for example, are not categorical desires, since we care only about fulfilling such desires on the condition that we are alive to fulfill them. Categorical desires, such as the desire that one's children do well after one dies, are not conditional in this sense and can thus provide a "purpose" to human lives. Elina's problem is that she has fulfilled all the categorical desires that gave her life meaning and can find no new ones to take their place. It is simply that "everything that could happen to one particular human being of forty-two had already happened to her."[14]

The problem with categorical desires, according to Williams, is that they eventually "dry up." The desire to successfully raise four or five (or ten or twenty) children might well provide meaning and purpose to a person's life. But what happens when one has raised hundreds of children over the course of thousands of years? It seems likely that, over an infinite expanse of time, many of us would find it difficult to hold on to the same attitude of hope and caring that we originally had. Nothing would be new or surprising. The same thing holds true for almost any categorical desire. One can only write so many books or compete in so many sporting events before one ceases to find such activities worthy of pursuit.

Aside from the Cullens, the lives of the *Twilight* vampires provide examples of a life without categorical desires. The vampires live for the gratification of immediate hungers and lusts; they rarely seem to care about things outside themselves. Even when they "love" one another, as Victoria and

James apparently do, this seems to be a mere desire to be in each other's company and not a genuine concern for each other. Moreover, this feature of immortals is not unique to the *Twilight* saga. Vampires generally are described as self-interested creatures driven by rage, lust, and hunger. The same holds true for the Greek and Roman gods, for Milton's rebellious angels, and for faeries and goblins throughout folklore. Immortals, with rare exceptions such as the Cullens, are regularly described as shortsighted and self-absorbed, with little interest in the values that shape human life.

It's Complicated

> You don't get to be human again, Bella. This is a once-in-a-lifetime shot.
>
> —Alice Cullen, *Eclipse*[15]

Now consider Bella's choice again. She is being offered immortal life with the promise that she can spend it with other immortals she loves. If Williams is right, Bella has every reason to expect that one day (perhaps thousands of years from now) she *will* have lost her categorical desires and will have become bored with her new life. When this day comes, it's unclear whether it will still be *Bella* making the choice to commit suicide or to continue on—after all, we are defined by those things that truly matter to us. Someone else in Bella's body, someone with the same memories but with none of Bella's categorical desires for the well-being of others, wouldn't be recognizable *as* Bella. Bella has no reason to expect that this creature will make the right choice; in fact, she has every reason to think that it will behave as badly as most vampires with similar desires do. This provides Bella with at least some reason to think that immortality might not be the right choice for *her*, even if the Volturi and others are perfectly content with it.

In the end, it's impossible to say whether Bella's love for Edward and others will be capable of providing meaning to her immortal existence. If Nussbaum and Williams are correct, however, it will be very difficult for an immortal creature to be capable of anything like a meaningful human life for an indefinite period of time. Our lives are given meaning by the people and causes we choose to sacrifice our time and effort to. Immortals, even in the limited sense in which vampires are immortal, might not have the same capacity to "sacrifice" anything. Even if Bella's love does survive the change unscathed, as it seems to, this ability may diminish with time, as the sheer repetitiveness of immortal life begins to take its toll. There is simply no way of telling for sure what such a life would be like.

Bella's choice is a version of the choice we all make in deciding how we ought to live our lives. It is tempting to think, as Bella initially seems to, that love is somehow "more than human" or that our mortality is an unfortunate accident that prevents us from fulfilling our duty to love one another. But actually our ability to love is closely tied to our mortality and vulnerability. We can love one another only so far as we are capable of sacrificing ourselves, and only when the person loved can in some way be helped by our sacrifice. Moreover, the desires and purposes that shape our lives may themselves necessarily be limited, incapable of being stretched out over an infinite existence. Bella's choice to become a vampire is not necessarily the wrong one for her to make, but it is not one that we should envy.

NOTES

1. Stephenie Meyer, *Twilight* (New York: Little, Brown and Company, 2005), p. 474.

2. Leo Tolstoy, "What Men Live By," in *What Men Live By and Other Tales*, trans. by Aylmer Maude and Louise Maude (Boston: The Stratford Company, 1918), p. 33.

3. *Twilight*, p. 476.

4. Ibid., p. 498.

5. Leo Tolstoy, *A Confession and Other Religious Writings*, trans. by Jane Kentish (London: Penguin Classics, 1988), p. 32.

6. *Twilight*, p. 473.

7. Lucretius, *On the Nature of the Universe*, trans. by Ronald Melville (New York: Oxford University Press, 2009), p. 92.

8. Stephenie Meyer, *New Moon* (New York: Little, Brown and Company, 2006), p. 518.

9. Stephenie Meyer, *Eclipse* (New York: Little, Brown and Company, 2007), p. 273.

10. Martha Nussbaum, "Mortal Immortals: Lucretius on Death and the Voice of Nature," *Philosophy and Phenomenological Research* 50 (1989), p. 337.

11. Nussbaum, "Mortal Immortals," p. 338.

12. Stephenie Meyer, *Breaking Dawn* (New York: Little, Brown and Company, 2008), p. 749.

13. Bernard Williams, "The Makropulos Case: Reflections on the Tedium of Immortality," in John Fisher (ed.), *The Metaphysics of Death* (Stanford, CA: Stanford University Press, 1993), p. 74.

14. Williams, "The Makropulos Case," p. 82.

15. *Eclipse*, p. 311.

seven

MIND READING AND MORALITY: THE MORAL HAZARDS OF BEING EDWARD

Eric Silverman

If you could do, have, or achieve virtually anything you desired, what goals would you pursue? Edward Cullen finds himself facing this very question. He has a very special gift in addition to the standard vampiric abilities such as immortality, extraordinary strength, and speed: Edward can read the minds of vampires and humans alike. While it is clear that Edward and the rest of the Cullen family seek to use their abilities in morally permissible ways, it is easy to overlook the special moral obligations entailed by this mind-reading talent.

Does Power Corrupt or Reveal Moral Character?

"He absolutely loathes me," Edward said cheerfully.

"You can't know that," I argued, but then I wondered suddenly if he could.

—*Twilight*[1]

Edward's gifts place him in a unique position. While most vampires at least fear that being discovered could force them to leave an area, Edward's mind-reading abilities allow him to do whatever he wishes with near impunity. Edward describes some of the advantages that mind reading allows: "I knew how to be charming when I wanted to be. It was easy, since I was able to know instantly how any tone or gesture was taken."[2] Knowing someone's thoughts gives access to the most useful and privileged kinds of information. Such information can enable all sorts of manipulation, deception, and other morally troubling activities. With his gift, Edward could do just about anything.

Along similar lines, the great philosopher Plato (428–348 BCE) wrote about the moral implications of possessing supernatural powers so great that they allow one to do absolutely anything. Plato claimed that such powers reveal one's "truest self." In Plato's story of the Ring of Gyges, a magic ring grants the power of invisibility, which would enable a person to do whatever he wishes without fearing consequences from being caught. Such abilities provide an ultimate test of character.

Plato rejected the idea that, as we might say today, "power corrupts." Instead he believed that power reveals a person's true character. While an unjust person would do evil, a truly just person would continue to do good despite the temptations of the ring. Like the ring of Gyges, Edward's mind-reading ability combined with his other powers enables him to do virtually whatever he wants. Not only can Edward kill or overpower others, but his mind-reading would enable him to conceal his actions, know others' secrets, and know if others even suspect him. His ability provides a test of character similar to the test provided by the Ring of Gyges.

Benevolence and Mind Reading

> From the time of my new birth . . . I had the advantage of knowing what everyone around me was thinking, both human and nonhuman alike.
>
> —Edward, *Twilight*[3]

Carlisle Cullen is quite aware of the moral implications of supernatural gifts. He speaks with moral clarity concerning the ethical implications of his own vampiric powers. Explaining his own attitude toward his abilities, he says, "Like everything in life, I just had to decide what to do with what I was given."[4] Serving as the "voice of morality" in the *Twilight* novels, Carlisle identifies a person's overarching goals as the central ethical question.

Accordingly, the first ethical question we should ask concerning mind reading focuses upon the overarching purposes Edward pursues with his gift. What distinguishes moral goals from immoral pursuits? One common principle claims that ethical actions are those intended to help others. Rather than focusing on our own happiness, the philosopher Immanuel Kant (1724–1804) argued, we have a central moral duty to seek the happiness of others: "When it comes to my promoting happiness as an end that is also a duty, this must therefore be the happiness of other human beings."[5] The common preoccupation with one's own happiness is a frequent source of moral failure. Kant described the condition of a person who fully embraces the pursuit of his own desires over the demands of morality as one of "radical evil."

While Kant believed that morality requires that people pursue the happiness of others, John Stuart Mill (1806–1873) went even further by making the morality of actions depend completely on the effects they have on people's happiness. If he is correct, then the morality of mind reading rests solely on the consequences it has on the happiness of everyone it affects. As he explained his central moral principle, "[The] 'greatest happiness principle' holds that actions are right in proportion as they tend to promote happiness; wrong as they tend to produce the reverse of happiness."[6] Mill viewed the morality of actions as entirely contingent on their effects on the lives they touch. Actions that advance the happiness of all are moral, while actions that undermine overall happiness are immoral.

Isabella Swan expresses a moral principle similar to Kant's and Mill's. She doesn't care whether her friends are vampires, werewolves, or humans, but she is greatly concerned about the effects their actions have on other people. For example, she assures her werewolf friend Jacob Black that she is not bothered by his shape-shifting; she is only concerned when his actions harm other people. As she explains, "No, Jake, no. It's not that you're a . . . wolf. That's fine. . . . If you could just find a way not to hurt people . . . that's all that upsets me."[7] Bella repeatedly demonstrates that she is undisturbed by her friends' powers whether they be strength, shape-shifting, or mind reading, but she is concerned when those abilities are used to harm others.

How benevolent is Edward's use of mind reading? Does he use it to advance everyone's happiness or only his own? In many cases, Edward clearly demonstrates benevolence toward others. Even before he abandoned the traditional vampire diet of human blood, he used mind reading to ensure that he harmed only truly evil humans and thereby advanced the overall good. He explains, "Because I knew the thoughts of my prey, I could pass over the innocent and pursue only the evil. If I followed a murderer down a dark alley where he stalked a young girl—if I saved her, then surely I wasn't so terrible. . . . But as time went on, I began to see the monster in my eyes. I couldn't escape the debt of so much human life taken, no matter how justified."[8] While Edward once saw some merit in directing his monstrous appetite toward violent criminals and thereby contributing to the overall happiness of society, he ultimately admits that taking a human life is inherently a serious matter and vigilante justice is morally dubious at best—especially when one desires to feed off the blood of the guilty. Such actions are hardly those of a morally ideal person.

Edward admirably uses his gifts to benefit his family, Bella, and others close to him, while hiding his vampiric identity for his family's sake. He uses his mind reading to protect Bella from potential rapists in Port Angeles, to protect her from hostile vampires like James and the Volturi, and to protect Bella's father, Charlie. Edward also uses his abilities to help protect other students from his brother Jasper Cullen's limited self-control. While Edward aids those close to him, however, morality requires more than benevolent concern for only close friends and family. Both Kant and Mill emphasized that we have moral obligations toward everyone, not just friends and family. So Edward's benevolence should extend to everyone in Forks and beyond. Instead, though, he regularly uses his abilities in manipulative ways with little care for how he affects others. For example, he frequently reads Charlie's mind in order to deceive him about aspects of his relationship with Bella, such as his frequent midnight visits to her room.

Unlike Carlisle, who actively serves others in Forks as a doctor, Edward does not seek to benefit others in general, but only those closest to him. He is content to focus his benevolence exclusively on his friends and family. His broader indifference toward others is morally troubling, though surely preferable to the predatory attitude that most vampires have toward humans.

Privacy and Mind Reading

I'm glad you can't read my thoughts. It's bad enough that you eavesdrop on my sleep-talking.

—Bella, *Twilight*[9]

While the benevolence of one's actions is an important moral test, there are additional principles to consider when examining the morality of mind reading. One important principle is the need to respect the autonomy and privacy of others.[10] Consider Charlie's violation of Bella's privacy as he opens her package from the University of Alaska Southeast.[11] Bella describes her negative reaction: "I flipped the envelope over and then glared up at him. 'It's open . . . I'm shocked, Sheriff. That's a federal crime.'" Why is she so offended? The problem is not that Charlie's motives are malicious. After all, he is driven by a genuine concern for Bella's welfare and even wants to pay her college tuition. Yet, the casual violation of her privacy demonstrates disrespect for Bella's autonomy. Mere curiosity is an insufficient reason for such an invasion of privacy, even with the best of intentions.

Yet, there are circumstances where someone might have an overriding moral justification for violating a moral principle. For example, Alice Cullen and Bella are morally justified in committing grand theft auto in order to save Edward's life in Italy. Similarly, sometimes an invasion of privacy can be morally justified. Charlie might have reasons of overwhelming importance that would justify an invasion of privacy. Suppose that he reads Bella's diary, not because he's worried about her in some vague sense, but because she is missing and he believes that reading her diary might help him find her. Such an overwhelming need for the information, combined with genuine benevolent concern for Bella, would justify an invasion of privacy.

What is so harmful about lack of privacy? Privacy and autonomy are directly connected to human well-being. Our secrets are among our most treasured possessions. Consider Bella's feelings of betrayal when Jacob reveals her motorcycling to Charlie. She explains, "The sting of betrayal washed through me. I had trusted Jacob implicitly—trusted him with every single secret I had."[12] Intimate knowledge of our selves, including our secrets, is like a kind of property to which others are not usually entitled. Accessing secrets or revealing them to others without an adequate reason is a kind of theft or betrayal.

Furthermore, it is simply embarrassing to have every thought involuntarily subject to the scrutiny of others. For example, Jacob shares some of the everyday pain caused by his telepathic link with the other werewolves. He explains that "we can hear . . . thoughts—each other's anyway—no matter how far away from each other we are. . . . It's embarrassing having no secrets like that."[13] Such harms are morally significant. The use of mind reading, then, needs an overriding moral justification.

One way to avoid a morally unacceptable invasion of privacy is to get consent before mind reading. For example, Aro asks permission before he attempts to read Bella's mind.[14] Yet, his "request" is not genuine because Bella has no real opportunity to reject his request. As she says, "My eyes flashed up to Edward's face in terror. Despite Aro's overt politeness, I didn't believe I really had a choice."[15] Aro's example demonstrates that "going through the motions" of asking permission is not enough to get real consent. Consent requires a genuine opportunity to reject such a request.

Moral mind reading requires both benevolent goals and either the genuine consent of the people whose minds are read or an overriding concern of very serious importance. Self-interest or curiosity is a morally inadequate justification for such an extreme invasion of privacy. These standards are easy for the mind reader to violate, however, since there is much one could gain from immoral mind reading and little danger of getting caught.

Does Edward limit his mind reading appropriately or does he ignore the boundaries of privacy? Edward claims that he typically avoids reading other people's minds. He tells Bella, "'Most of the time, I tune it all out—it can be very distracting. And then it's easier to seem *normal*'—he frowned as he said the word—'when I'm not answering someone's thoughts rather than their words.'"[16] While it is praiseworthy that Edward does not constantly use his abilities out of mere curiosity, his reasons are fairly self-interested. He is motivated by the personal inconveniences that come from mind reading rather than a concern for others' privacy. Edward himself admits, "Only four voices did I block out of courtesy rather than distaste: my family. . . . I gave them what privacy I could. I tried not to listen if I could help it."[17] As with most of his other benevolent actions, Edward respects the privacy of his close friends and family as a matter of principle, but is indifferent toward other people more generally.

Furthermore, there are plenty of times when Edward is willing to violate others' privacy. For example, although he cannot read Bella's mind, he actively spies on her, even in her sleep.[18] He reads her friends' minds simply to keep track of her;[19] he reads her friends' minds to see if she keeps her promise not to tell anyone about his unusual speed and strength; he seems to have used his ability to confirm Mike Newton's negative feelings about him; and he desires to read Bella's thoughts for his own comfort.[20] Of course, some of these invasions of privacy are justifiable. He keeps track of Bella in Port Angeles to protect her, and it enables him to save her life.[21] His mind reading allows him to anticipate Jasper's reflexive attack on Bella when he smells her blood.[22] He reads the minds of the Volturi in order to protect the lives of Alice, Bella, and himself.[23] But some of his mind reading is not ultimately justifiable.

Let's raise one final consideration concerning Edward's mind reading. Unlike many invasions of privacy, such as reading another person's diary, mind reading isn't completely voluntary. As with any other sense, Edward can try to avoid using it or ignore it, but he cannot simply turn it off. This fact is important because only voluntary actions have moral implications. For example, Kant famously claimed that "ought implies can."[24] Any genuine moral obligation must be within a person's ability to carry out. Similarly, Aristotle acknowledged that choice "is felt to be very closely related to moral goodness, and to be a better test of character than actions are."[25] Aristotle believed that actions that are not truly chosen are not a good test of character. Therefore, to the degree that Edward's mind reading is involuntary, he cannot be obligated to avoid using it. While this factor mitigates some of his responsibility, it is clear that there are many times when his invasion of others' privacy is both deliberate and unjustified.

Love and the Inequality of Mind Reading

It's too easy to be myself with you. . . . Tell me what you're thinking. . . . It's still so strange for me, not knowing.

—Edward, *Twilight*[26]

Edward's relationship with Bella is largely shaped by his inability to read her mind, allowing for a greater equality between them. While Bella is still "merely human" throughout much of their relationship, the inequality between them is not as great as it would have been if he constantly invaded her privacy through mind reading. Furthermore, love is strengthened by an element of mystery, and much of Bella's mystery would be lost through mind reading.

Similarly, Aristotle claimed that the best relationships require a type of equality and that radical inequalities undermine relationships. "This becomes evident if a wide gap develops between the parties in respect of virtue or vice, or of affluence or anything else; because they no longer remain friends, and do not even expect to do so."[27] Accordingly, Bella is aware that vast inequalities within a relationship create obstacles that are difficult to overcome. She describes the nature of her love for Edward and the tension between her appreciation of his best qualities and the challenge created by the inequalities, saying, "I love *him*. Not because he's beautiful or because he's *rich*. . . . I'd much rather he weren't either one. It would even out the gap between us just a little bit— because he'd still be the most loving and unselfish and brilliant and *decent* person I've ever met."[28]

Bella echoes two Aristotelian themes. First, that the best types of relationships are founded upon the mutual appreciation of shared virtue. Bella's love is based on her admiration of Edward's character, not his wealth or beauty. Second, she recognizes that inequalities in a relationship can create a "gap" that can be difficult to overcome. Since Edward's money and beauty are additional sources of inequality in their relationship, Bella views them as obstacles for their relationship, rather than the source of her love. If Edward could read her mind and further add to the inequalities in the relationship, his ability would create an even more serious distance between them. Bella's immunity to mind reading makes her more equal to him and therefore a better candidate for the best kind of relationship.

God and Morality

But never, in the nearly four hundred years now since
I was born, have I ever seen anything to make me
doubt whether God exists in some form or the other.

—Carlisle, *New Moon*[29]

An overarching religious motif runs throughout the *Twilight*
series, beginning on the page before the start of the first book,
as it cites the warning of Genesis 2:17: "But of the tree of the
knowledge of good and evil, thou shalt not eat of it: for in the day
that thou eatest thereof thou shalt surely die."

What is it about religious faith that drives some of the
most admirable people in their actions? Obviously, there is
a kind of religious faith that is destructive and immoral, as
exemplified by Carlisle's father, who was driven to violence
by his imbalanced faith. Yet, despite the negative aspects of
his religious upbringing, Carlisle's rejection of the typical
vampire lifestyle and desire for moral enlightenment are ultimately driven by his faith in God.[30]

Similarly, religious faith plays an important role in the
moral lives of many people. Kant went so far as to suggest that
faith in the existence of God, the soul, and the afterlife were
prerequisites for a successful moral life. He claimed that the
successful moral life requires that one must believe in the possibility of "happiness proportioned to [one's degree of virtue] . . .
it must lead to the supposition of the existence of a cause adequate to this effect; in other words, it must postulate the existence of God."[31] Kant claimed that rationality itself demands
that humanity pursue the greatest good, which includes happiness distributed throughout the world in proportion to moral
worth. Yet, he argued that pursuing the greatest good requires
believing that the greatest good is really possible. Therefore,
the successful moral life demands belief in the existence of

everything necessary for accomplishing the greatest good, such as God. Kant concluded that "it is not merely allowable, but is a necessity connected with duty as a requisite. . . . [I]t is morally necessary to assume the existence of God."[32]

Although Edward seems to reject Carlisle's faith, some of his actions suggest that his rejection is halfhearted. Most notably, his repeated refusal to transform Bella into a vampire is driven by a concern that doing so would destroy her soul.[33] Similarly, when he sees Bella after he thinks she has died, he responds with a religious interpretation when he says in surprise, "Carlisle was right."[34] While Edward's use of mind reading and his other vampiric powers falls short of ideal, he repeatedly demonstrates a desire to overcome his own violent nature and to help those close to himself. Perhaps it is this latent faith that helps him exercise restraint with mind reading and his other vampiric abilities.

One Last Thought before Dawn

Despite Bella's adoring evaluation of Edward's morality, we have demonstrated that he remains a morally flawed person. Still, he certainly aspires to transcend his nature, his circumstances, and his own limitations. He seeks to become a better person, despite his current moral flaws. These aspirations make Edward's character more "human" and make it easier for all of us to relate to him. In the end, it is the very combination of Edward's moral imperfections along with his moral aspirations that make his story so attractive, intriguing, and compelling.

NOTES

1. Stephenie Meyer, *Twilight* (New York: Little, Brown and Company, 2005), p. 99.

2. Stephenie Meyer, *Midnight Sun* (partial draft), www.stepheniemeyer.com/pdf/midnightsun_partial_draft4.pdf, p. 19.

3. *Twilight*, p. 342.

4. Stephenie Meyer, *New Moon* (New York: Little, Brown and Company, 2006), p. 35.

5. Immanuel Kant, *Metaphysics of Morals*, Mary Gregor (ed.) (Glasgow: Cambridge University Press, 1996), p. 151. (6:388).

6. John Stuart Mill, *Utilitarianism*, 2nd ed., George Sher (ed.), (Indianapolis, IN: Hackett Publishing Company, 2001), p. 7.

7. *New Moon*, pp. 307–308.

8. *Twilight*, p. 343.

9. Ibid., p. 309.

10. See W. A. Parent, "Privacy, Morality, and the Law," *Philosophy and Public Affairs* 12.4 (1983), pp. 269–288.

11. Stephenie Meyer, *Eclipse* (New York: Little, Brown and Company, 2007), p. 15.

12. *New Moon*, p. 553.

13. Ibid., p. 317.

14. Ibid., p. 473.

15. Ibid., p. 473.

16. *Twilight*, p. 180.

17. *Midnight Sun*, p. 1.

18. *Twilight*, p. 309.

19. Ibid., p. 176.

20. Ibid., pp. 99, 273, 309.

21. Ibid., p. 174.

22. *New Moon*, p. 28.

23. Ibid., p. 532.

24. See Immanuel Kant, *Critique of Pure Reason*, trans. by Norman Kemp Smith (New York: St. Martin's Press, 1965), p. 637 (A807, B835).

25. Aristotle, *The Ethics of Aristotle: The Nicomachean Ethics*, trans. by J. A. K. Thompson (New York: Penguin Books, 1976), p. 116 (1111b).

26. *Twilight*, p. 262.

27. Aristotle, *Ethics of Aristotle*, p. 270 (1158b).

28. *Eclipse*, p. 110.

29. *New Moon*, p. 36.

30. Ibid., p. 36.

31. Immanuel Kant, *Critique of Practical Reason*, trans. by T. K. Abbott (Amherst, NY: Prometheus Books, 1996), p. 150.

32. Ibid., p. 152.

33. *New Moon*, p. 37.

34. Ibid., p. 452.

eight

LOVE AND AUTHORITY AMONG WOLVES

Sara Worley

When Sam Uley imprints on Emily Young, he hurts Leah Clearwater deeply. But does he have any control over this? Can he help himself? Should we blame him? Jacob Black imprints on Renesmee, and in doing so, changes his whole life and the life of the pack. How is this different from what happens when a human falls in love? When Sam gives a command, the pack has to obey. How different is this from the kind of authority that a general has over his troops?

As these questions suggest, the *Twilight* books raise a number of issues about free will. Most of us think we have free will, in that what we do is up to us. No matter what we do, we could always have done something else instead. Our ability to make free decisions is why Alice Cullen's visions about the future are not always reliable, or even available. They are not reliable when what's going to happen in the future depends on the decisions that someone is going to make, because anyone who makes a decision can always change his or her mind and do something else instead. And when a decision hasn't been made yet, then Alice can't see it at all.[1]

But wolves don't seem free to do something other than what they actually do. When Sam decides that the pack must attack Bella Swan's unborn child, Jacob does not want to obey. He thinks Sam's decision is wrong. But (at least before he claims his rightful authority as alpha), he seems to have no choice.[2] This, of course, is totally different from what happens when a superior officer in the army gives an order. A soldier may want to obey so that he doesn't get punished. He may want to obey because he thinks obeying the commands of his superior officer is the right thing to do. But it's still his choice. If he really thought the command was wrong, or immoral, he could refuse to obey it and suffer the consequences. Jacob doesn't seem to have this option. He has no choice about whether to obey.

Imprinting doesn't seem any better. When Sam imprinted on Emily, he couldn't have done otherwise. (Indeed, it seems likely that if he had a choice about it, he wouldn't have done it, given how much he hurt Leah.)[3] Jacob certainly wouldn't have chosen to imprint on Renesmee, given how he felt about the vampires, and about Bella, but it happened anyway. Not only that, but once a wolf imprints, he doesn't seem to have much control over his behavior.

Suppose that a woman who's married and has children falls in love with someone else. We might think that even if she doesn't have a choice about whether she falls in love, she surely has a choice about how she behaves. She can choose to leave her husband and family because her new love is more important to her. She might think that her children will adjust in the long run, and that they will be happier if she is happy. Or she might choose to stay with her husband and children because she values above anything the commitment she made to her husband. Or she might think that breaking up her marriage would be damaging to her children. Whatever she decides, she has a choice. The fact that she's fallen in love doesn't dictate how she'll behave.

The wolves don't seem to have the same choice. Sam is presented throughout as someone who values his commitments. He certainly takes his commitment to the pack seriously. Once he imprints on Emily, however, he doesn't seem to have a choice about what to do. He can't decide that his commitment to Leah is more important than his attraction to Emily. How he behaves is not really up to him.

What's Free Will, Anyway?

Maybe there's a better way to understand free will. A soldier's decision to obey his superior officer seems free, because it seems that he could have done otherwise. He could have refused, if he had been willing to pay the consequences. But is it really so obvious that he could have done otherwise? Many philosophers have concluded that what a person does in a given situation depends on the beliefs and desires that person has.[4]

Suppose that Bella's friend Angela Weber is really hungry and goes to a party where there's a variety of good food. If she thinks that she's not going to be near any other food for the rest of the evening, she's probably going to eat. If she doesn't eat, it must be because she has some other good reason for not eating. Maybe she thinks the food is poisoned, or maybe she'd rather dance than eat. Maybe she's on a diet. Whatever she does will depend on her beliefs (such as whether she will get food later, or whether the food is poisoned) and her desires (such as whether she wants to lose weight, or whether she would rather dance than eat). If she wants food more than she wants anything else at the moment, and she doesn't have any good reason not to eat, then she will eat.

So what we do depends on what our strongest desire is. Not only that, but we don't always have control over what our desires are. Bella desires human food and sleep because she is a human being, and all humans desire those things. Vampires desire human blood instead of human food because they are, well, vampires. Other desires can be traced to our culture or the environment in which we live, or to the fact that we were raised a certain way. When Carlisle Cullen was growing up, his father was strongly anti-vampire. Surely this is part of the reason that Carlisle reacted the way he did when he was first bit.[5]

Now, of course, sometimes people change their desires, or their beliefs. Bella didn't always want to be a vampire. She doesn't acquire this desire because of the way she was raised, or because of her human nature. So it looks like she chooses to have this desire. But it's not quite so simple. One of the main things motivating her to want to become a vampire is the fear that her human existence is putting everyone she loves at risk. Victoria is a threat to Charlie and to any of the wolves or vampires who might fight her. The Volturi are an even bigger threat. And the only way to remove these threats is for Bella to become a vampire herself. So she has good reasons for acquiring the desire to become a vampire.[6] It's not just out of the blue. And the love for her family and friends, and the desire to protect them that motivates her to become a vampire, are also not out of the blue. She is concerned about protecting her family and friends because she is the kind of person she is, who had the kind of upbringing she did. (She is also motivated to become a vampire, of course, because she doesn't want to age while Edward stays young forever. There's also presumably a reason that this matters so much to her!)

So perhaps the lesson we should learn from all this is that nobody really has free will. Some philosophers have thought that this is true, and that free will is just an illusion.[7] But other philosophers have had a different response. Free will, for them, has nothing to do with whether you could do otherwise. It has to do, instead, with whether you approve of or endorse the desires that cause your behavior. Contemporary philosopher Harry Frankfurt provides one of the most compelling versions of this theory.[8] Frankfurt's idea is that most of us have conflicting desires. We endorse some of these desires, and we don't endorse others. We want our behavior to be caused by those desires we endorse, rather than by those desires that we don't approve of. We're free to the extent that our behavior is caused by the desires that we endorse.

The Cullens are a good example of this kind of freedom. Since they are vampires, they all thirst for human blood. When Bella bleeds in their presence, they have to cover their noses, refrain from breathing, or leave the room. (Carlisle is an exception to this, since he has the desire remarkably under control.) Yet they do not endorse this desire or the behavior that it produces. They don't want to take innocent human life to quench their thirst. So they choose not to satisfy their thirst, precisely because not satisfying it is a way of achieving a kind of moral life, which is what they value. So based on this concept of free will, they are free. Indeed, if they value morality highly enough, perhaps they aren't able to do otherwise. The Cullens are free because their behavior is governed by the desires they value, rather than those they reject. Instead of being slaves to their desire for blood, they are the masters of it.

The Cullens would lack free will if they ever gave in to their desire for blood; doing so would conflict with things they value more highly, such as human life. Rosalie Cullen provides a nice example of this. She looks forward to the birth of Bella's child almost as much as Bella does. A theme throughout is how much she grieves over not having been able to have her own child and how much she resents Bella for (apparently) choosing to throw away the chance to live a normal human life and have a child of her own. Yet when the child is on the verge of being born, Rosalie almost loses control of her thirst, putting Bella's life, and presumably the life of the child, at risk.[9] Causing the death of the child would be just about the worst thing from Rosalie's perspective, yet she risks doing so because she loses self-control. She becomes a slave to her desire, rather than its master.

The Wolves, Free Will, and Authority

What, then, should we conclude about the wolves? Does this new concept of freedom change our views about whether the wolves are free? To be free is to have your behavior governed by those desires you endorse, or want to be motivated by. The authority of the alphas still doesn't pass this test. When Sam decides that the pack should attack Bella's child, Jacob doesn't think that this is right. He thinks that Sam is making a mistake. Indeed, he thinks that attacking the Cullens would be immoral. But these concerns make no difference. While Jacob is still under Sam's authority, he is not able to act on his own judgment about what should be done. He doesn't approve, but his lack of approval makes no difference.

The only reason Jacob is able to resist is that he seizes his authority as the rightful alpha. Note what goes on here. It's not simply that Jacob realizes that he doesn't have to obey. One can imagine this in the case of a human authority figure. Suppose that, say, a religious authority figure—a priest or a rabbi—asks you to do something that you don't think is right. You might nonetheless think that you should obey, because after all, the priest or rabbi has authority over you. But then suppose that you come to realize that the authority figure is not really legitimate after all (suppose it's a priest who has been defrocked). Then, once you realize that the priest is not really a priest anymore and doesn't have any legitimate authority, you might change your mind about whether you have to obey.

This is not what happens with Jacob, however. Rather, the transformation is almost magical. Once Jacob seizes his rightful authority, Sam loses his ability to command him. It's not just that Jacob has decided that he doesn't have to obey. Rather, assuming his proper authority seems to have a kind of magical power, which removes the influence that Sam's commands have over his body. And indeed, the magical difference extends to the other wolves, who are now free to decide which pack to join. There is little question that this is only made possible because Jacob is in fact the rightful alpha. Without that, none of them would have had the capacity to act according to their own judgment.[10]

Wolf Love and Free Will

Imprinting, however, is a different story. It's no doubt true that the wolves don't have any control over whether, or on whom, they imprint. The question, though, is whether their behavior is governed by desires they endorse or by desires they reject. Or to put it another way, could the wolves resist the desires caused by imprinting (as the Cullens resist the desire for blood), in case these desires conflict with something that they value more highly? Could a wolf ever behave in a way that is detrimental to the happiness or well-being of the beloved? Could Jacob have sacrificed Renesmee if he thought she was genuinely a threat to the human community, or to other things that he holds dear? Could Jacob leave for good if he thought his presence was not in Renesmee's best interest in the long run? Or does the imprinting absolutely control what wolves do, no matter what else they believe or value? Are they slaves to their imprinting, or are they its master?

Meyer doesn't quite give us enough evidence to fully answer these questions, but there are clues. The first clue comes from Sam. Sam is the kind of person who values his commitments and loyalties highly, and he doesn't want to hurt Leah. But none of this makes any difference. Once he imprints on Emily, he is bound to hurt Leah, no matter what his other values or commitments are. So perhaps the imprinting governs his behavior, even though the behavior conflicts with his other values.

The situation is more complicated than this, however. Sam has other commitments that he continues to respect. He's committed to the well-being of the pack, and he's committed to ensuring the well-being of the humans that he's sworn to protect. And he doesn't seem to have a problem balancing these commitments against the desires caused by his imprinting on Emily. Fighting vampires is dangerous work. Any harm to Sam would no doubt cause Emily great suffering. Nonetheless, Sam doesn't seem to have any trouble putting his obligations to pack and human community first. He is not so compelled by his attraction to Emily that he is incapable of fulfilling his other responsibilities.

All of this, however, might not actually show that wolves have free will. Perhaps part of their "wolfy" nature is that the satisfaction of their protection duties comes first, and nothing else can interfere with this. Perhaps the desires associated with imprinting come second. In neither case, however, would the wolves really be free, because in neither case would any other commitments or obligations have a chance. The wolves would have to protect the community, and the wolves would have to look after the interests of their beloved, no matter what else a particular wolf might happen to value or care about. But even if this is correct, it wouldn't show that the wolves are not free.

At the beginning of the Protestant Reformation, when Martin Luther was formulating a set of challenges to the Roman Catholic Church, he famously said, "Here I stand: I can do no other."[11] Luther was suggesting that his commitment was so strong that he could not violate it—there was nothing else that mattered so much to him. He was not claiming that his act was not free. Indeed, on Frankfurt's analysis, the question of whether Luther had free will is the question of whether he could have refrained from posing his challenges, had he decided that challenging the Church was not a good idea. And, of course, he could have. He wasn't compelled to pose his challenges no matter what else he believed. The claim that he could do no other doesn't indicate any sort of compulsion; it emphasizes the strength of his convictions.

Imprinting doesn't just produce new desires; it also produces new values. An imprinted wolf not only comes to desire spending time with and ensuring the well-being of his beloved, but comes to endorse, or value, these desires as well. Furthermore, any conflicting desires lose their importance. This is not what happens with the vampires. When they become transformed, they acquire a taste for human blood. But at least for some of them, this isn't accompanied by a change in their moral outlook. They don't also begin to believe that taking innocent human life is a good thing. So acquiring the desire for blood doesn't affect their values, or affect which desires they consider worthy of endorsement. But for the wolves, something like this value change does seem to happen upon imprinting. Not only does an imprinted wolf come to desire the well-being of the beloved, but the wolf endorses that desire. That desire becomes the thing the wolf most values (or at least one of the things that the wolf most values), and anything that conflicts with it loses its importance.

So does Sam hurt Leah? Yes. Is he the sort of person who values his commitments? Yes. But this doesn't mean that his behavior is not free. So what happened when he imprinted? His desire not to hurt Leah became less important than his desire to be with Emily. He wasn't a slave to his new desire, because to be a slave to a desire is to have to satisfy it, even if satisfying it costs you things that you value more. Rosalie would have been a slave to her desire if she had given in to it even though doing so would have cost her what she most valued. But Sam is not a slave to his desire, because although he does not relish hurting Leah, his desire not to hurt her becomes less important to him than his desire to be with Emily. He isn't acting out of a desire that he doesn't endorse. Rather, the imprinting causes him to endorse, or value, his desire to be with Emily, and makes his desire to avoid hurting Leah less important to him.

Of course, this change in values doesn't mean that every other commitment disappears, or becomes less valuable. Jacob still loves Billy, even though he's imprinted on Renesmee. He also still loves Bella, although not in the same way. He still values his friendships with Seth Clearwater, Quil Ateara, and Embry Call. And Sam, as we have seen, still values his commitment to the pack, and to protecting the human community. But imprinting does change values that conflict with the imprinting.

A Final Worry

There's one final worry: this sort of change in values brought about by imprinting might itself seem to conflict with free will. Usually, when people change their minds about something, they have had an opportunity to reflect on the change. They've had a chance to endorse or reject the new idea or value, depending on how it fits in with or conflicts with other things they believe. But this is precisely what *doesn't* happen in the case of imprinting. The change in values just happens, out of the blue. And it seems this should be a violation of one's free will. If someone implanted a chip in your brain that made you care about things that you totally hadn't cared about before, you would think that your free will had been violated. And this doesn't seem all that far from what happens in the case of imprinting.

But such a scenario isn't as clear-cut as it initially appears, even in the human case. Bella's immediate response to her pregnancy is to become concerned with her child's well-being. She's unwilling to do anything that might endanger the child, even at the risk of her own life. She's even willing to do things (like drink blood) that would have been repellent to her in her earlier life. This change is also from out of the blue. Bella hasn't reflected on it, or had the chance to reject it or endorse it. Yet this doesn't seem to involve any violation of free will. We can agree with Carlisle that the only violation of free will here would be the attempt to make Bella give up the child.[12] To do so would be to try to make her act against what are now her deepest values and commitments, even though she hasn't really chosen them.

Here Jacob Stands: He Can Do No Other

So could Jacob leave Renesmee, as Edward left Bella, if he came to believe that doing so was best for her? Could he have sacrificed her, if she had turned out to be a real danger to other people he loved? We cannot answer these questions with any confidence, because we really don't know enough about the other commitments that Jacob has, or the circumstances in which he would have to act. Even if the answer to these questions is no, that wouldn't by itself show that imprinted wolves have no free will. It might just show that Jacob, like Luther, could do no other.

NOTES

1. Stephenie Meyer, *New Moon* (New York: Little, Brown and Company, 2006), pp. 425–442.

2. Stephenie Meyer, *Breaking Dawn* (New York: Little, Brown and Company, 2008), pp. 202–211.

3. Stephenie Meyer, *Eclipse* (New York: Little, Brown and Company, 2007), pp. 122–123.

4. John Stuart Mill, *A System of Logic*, 8th ed. (New York: Harper & Brothers, 1874). Reprinted in James Hartman (ed.), *Philosophy of Recent Times*, vol. 1 (New York: McGraw Hill, 1967), pp. 198–203.

5. Stephenie Meyer, *Twilight* (New York: Little, Brown and Company, 2005), pp. 331–337.

6. *New Moon*, pp. 530–536.

7. See, for example, Ted Honderich, *How Free Are You: The Determinism Problem* (New York: Oxford University Press, 1993); and Brand Blanshard, "The Case for Determinism," in Neill Campbell ed., *Freedom, Determinism, and Responsibility: Readings in Metaphysics* (Upper Saddle River, NJ: Prentice Hall, 2003), pp. 7–15.

8. Harry Frankfurt, "Freedom of the Will and the Concept of a Person," *Journal of Philosophy* 68 (January 1971), pp. 5–20.

9. *Breaking Dawn*, p. 350.

10. Ibid., pp. 206–214.

11. This case is discussed in Dan Dennett, *Elbow Room: The Varieties of Free Will Worth Wanting* (Cambridge, MA: Bradford Books, 1984), p. 133.

12. *Breaking Dawn*, p. 234.

PART THREE

ECLIPSE

BELLA SWAN AND SARAH PALIN: ALL THE OLD MYTHS ARE *NOT* TRUE

Naomi Zack

Having It *All*

The four volumes of *Twilight* support a coherent narrative of development and transformation, from a classic situation of a young girl in love with a wonderful older man, into a mature relationship of full equality. Thus at the outset, Edward Cullen, who was born in 1901, far exceeds the contemporary high school student and mortal, Bella Swan, in mental and physical talents. He is also more beautiful than she. By the end of the fourth volume, however, Bella, as a newborn vampire, is physically stronger than Edward, just as mentally acute, and at least as beautiful.

From Bella's point of view, Edward changes from an exalted all-loving, all-knowing, and all-powerful demigod, to a devoted lover and husband, whom she is able to protect with her own special gift of psychic shielding. Edward admires and supports every stage of Bella's coming into her own powers, and is even able to accept the love of both Bella and their daughter for Jacob Black, the werewolf/"shape-shifter," whom Edward earlier despised. Edward is very much the new sensitive and caring man to Bella's new able, powerful, and courageous woman. He is even a so-called vegetarian vampire who kills animals for their blood instead of preying on humans.

Every Western ideal of romantic love and the contemporary success of heterosexual women is thereby fulfilled for the heroine of *Twilight*: She marries the vampire she loves and thereby joins a rich, cultured, and loving extended family, after which she skips through pregnancy in a couple of months, becomes a vampire to save her life, and attains the powers of a superheroine. Talk about "what women want!" If escape fiction as riveting as *Twilight* is really about our own mundane life and times—which I assume it is—then its fantastical elements may pinpoint exactly what young women aspire to in "having it all." (Or else, *Twilight* is a sublime send-up of the notion of having it all, although the author gives no indication of that.)

All of the Myths Are True

The most fantastical element of the *Twilight* quartet is not so much its content, which the reader accepts as a basic premise, but Bella's frequent pronouncement that all of the old myths are true. This self-reflexive incantation deftly connects the world of vampires and werewolves to everyday life, making it easy for the reader to vicariously live the story as her own mundane, mortal self. And so, the genre of children's fairy tales is thereby harnessed to the desires, yearnings, and aspirations of women in the early twenty-first century.

For although the *Twilight* series is categorized as reading for young adults, Stephenie Meyer has reported getting fan mail from women in their thirties—and they in turn may be the "scouts" for their older sisters, mothers, and grandmothers.

Consider Sarah Palin

If I were a conspiracy theorist, I would suggest that Bella softened up many young white women for Sarah Palin, because the series had already sold millions when Palin began to campaign with presidential candidate John McCain in fall 2008. However, at this writing, Bella seems to have greater staying power than Sarah Palin, insofar as Palin's team lost and Bella has been reincarnated in the movies. We should remember, though, that Palin retreated to Alaska, where she remained governor of an energy-rich state until she announced her resignation in July 2009. So in the long term, her assault on reality may turn out to be just as triumphant as Bella's.

A Lesson for Serious Feminists

Self-styled serious feminists have much to learn from these two mass heroines, who can only be dismissed if one ignores the yearnings of existing women. The *Twilight* books have sold twenty million copies and the first movie grossed $150 million in less than a month. Fifty million people voted for McCain-Palin, a number that was roughly half of the electorate, despite Barack Obama's landslide in the electoral college and an additional three million votes.[1] Both Bella and Palin offer clues about how the dreams of contemporary young women are historically innocent to the point of complete ignorance. Indeed, the absence of history in both trajectories is perhaps the most striking fact about them. For example, in the *Twilight* quartet, Jacob Black, the Native American shape-shifting character, lives in LaPush, Washington, which is the name of a real place, where the Quileute tribe has lived for at least eight hundred years. But nowhere in the *Twilight* publicity were these real people acknowledged, and so far as I know, no attempt has been made to recognize the literary license taken with their identities. Similarly, in Palin's acceptance speech at the Republican National Convention, Palin generously referred to the North Slope of Alaska as a source of still-untapped natural resources, in a manner that suggested she was completely oblivious of the effects of further drilling on natural habitats, ancestral indigenous lands, or global warming.

It is difficult to avoid the judgment that both Bella and Palin are American primitives, if not savages. Consider the picture of Palin (well circulated online during the fall of 2008) kneeling with one of her young daughters, behind a moose she had just shot.[2] Their expressions are cheerful and matter-of-fact. This picture is uncannily reminiscent of a scene from the last *Twilight* novel, when Bella, with her young daughter nearby, is interrupted while drinking the blood of a moose. (It should go without saying that when Bella becomes a vampire, she adopts the so-called vegetarian practices of her husband and his family.)

Ordinary women identify with Bella and Palin. Bella's mind is very accessible, because most of the events in the four novels are presented in the first person by her. Less is known about Palin's inner life, but her fans have no trouble in identifying with her, based primarily, it would seem, on her successful heterosexuality and working-class background. In these current female versions of Horatio Alger, successful upward social mobility is a broad prize, not unlike the imagined joy of winning the lottery. What is important to multitudes is being able to identify with where the heroine starts out. The prizes she gets need not be either earned or deserved. It is sufficient if those who identify with her would value the same prizes. On this note, while critics who never liked Palin to begin with might make much of the hypocrisy involved in her $150,000-plus makeover, it is unlikely to perturb supporters, who may themselves have developed similar aspirations from watching early twenty-first-century makeover shows on television.

What, you may ask, is the feminist point of all this? The point is that serious scholarly feminists seem not to be aware that these three things are very important to a majority of young American women: practicing heterosexuality in the form of fulfilled romantic love and fertility; looking good according to the prevailing beauty norms of consumer culture; and attaining power in the world as it is, rather than the world as it should be. The good news is that these values and aspirations do not appear or feel like the psychic attitudes of an oppressed and exploited gender. The bad news is that this idealized configuration is not accessible to all members of the female mass, almost by definition: The chances of the majority of female teenagers finding true love with vampires, or of becoming governors of a state after they are beauty queens, are next to zero. The question is whether feminists ought to further distance themselves from existing women by repudiating idealized heterosexuality, objectified beauty, and male-identified power for women; or if they should make a more conscientious attempt to at least bridge their culture gap with the masses.

Who Are the Real Elitists?

Contemporary feminists are not alone in their elitist doctrinal purity. As philosopher Richard Rorty (1931–2007) pointed out, there is a persistent and unacknowledged problem with how class is dealt with in higher education. He wrote:

> It seems to me that the regulative idea that we heirs of
> the Enlightenment, we Socratists, most frequently use

to criticize the conduct of various conversational partners is that of "needing education in order to outgrow their primitive fear, hatreds, and superstitions." . . . [S]tudents who enter as bigoted, homophobic, religious fundamentalists will leave college with views more like our own. . . . The fundamentalist parents of our fundamentalist students think that the entire "American liberal establishment" is engaged in a conspiracy. The parents have a point. Their point is that we liberal teachers no more feel in a symmetrical communication situation when we talk with bigots than do kindergarten teachers talking with their students . . . we do not consider the possibility of reformulating our own practices of justification so as to give more weight to the authority of the Christian scriptures. Instead, we do our best to convince these students of the benefits of secularization. We assign first-person accounts of growing up homosexual to our homophobic students for the same reasons that German schoolteachers in the postwar period assigned *The Diary of Anne Frank.* You have to be educated in order to be . . . a participant in our conversation. . . . So we are going to go right on trying to discredit you in the eyes of your children, trying to strip your fundamentalist religious community of dignity, trying to make your views seem silly rather than discussable. We are not so inclusivist as to tolerate intolerance such as yours.[3]

"We are not so inclusivist as to tolerate intolerance such as yours" could be rephrased by many intellectual feminists as: "We are not so pro-women as to tolerate the values of women such as you." And more specifically, we might add that contrary to what some in the mass media proclaimed, Palin is no more a real feminist than Bella is a real vegetarian. Behind such harsh rhetoric is a concern not for words but for what they stand for. Vegetarianism stands for not eating animals, and feminism stands for the interests of women and not merely their sexual or gendered identities. That is, since most of us already do not eat human flesh, it is a strange appropriation of the practice of those who already do not eat animal flesh to use the term "vegetarianism" as a positive label for those who abstain only from human flesh. And insofar as feminists, who have mostly been women, have fought long and hard for recognition of a right to choose abortion, as well as for recognition of the value of natural environments, it is a strange appropriation of feminism to contract its meaning to gender alone, so that it can be applied to someone who is militantly prolife and aggressively exploitative of nature.

The interests of women consist of social goals that would benefit large numbers of women in more or less equal ways. The error of the Bella and Palin fans is less in the content of their aspirations but in the inherent elitism of those aspirations. How many vampires could the Pacific Northwest support, without a significant decrease in the human, if not the animal, population? And as posed, how many women can be beauty queens, mothers of five, and governors of states, while running for vice president and possibly president after that, not to mention also modeling new wardrobes that cost hundreds of thousands of dollars? The point is that the lifestyles of Bella and Palin are not sustainable on a mass level. The contradiction inherent in their mass admiration is that all of their fans, who are their fans because they want what they have, cannot all have what they have.

Rorty is mistaken if he is implying that the important difference between American fundamentalists and the college professors who educate their children is the content of their ideas or how they justify them. The important difference would have to lie in their life values, insofar as those values structure how they live and enable others to live the same way. Or in other words, do American Christian fundamentalists have sustainable lifestyles, capable of including multitudes on an egalitarian basis? Their homophobia and strong prolife positions alone would seem to exclude the well-being of a significant number of their very own children.

So how can intellectual feminists bridge their gap from those young women who aspire to have what Bella and Palin are presented as having? First, I think it important to engage those mass views and ideals that are strongly opposed to one's own and try to analyze what is important and pleasurable about them to those who hold them (the compassionate move). Second, I think it's necessary to distinguish between views and ideals that are salient only for individuals in independent, exceptional, and possibly isolated ways, and views and ideals that within them include the well-being of multitudes (the Kantian move). Third, I think it's necessary to ask individuals to consider how their views and ideals are realized in their own lives and what practical steps it is possible for them to take to attain their ideals (the pragmatic move).

A Lesson for Feminists

The most telling lesson of Sarah Palin's success for feminists is that gender inclusivity alone at this point barely registers as a political goal. What does and should register is group interests that political candidates and officials represent and seek to further. Until scholarly feminists succeed in broadly explaining to women what their common interests as women are, everything that they have worked for is vulnerable to being stifled by having its label "borrowed" by those who serve goals that are not in the common interests of women. The lesson for feminists in Stephenie Meyer's success is that young women do want it all, and unless these young women are painstakingly taught that all the old myths are not true, they will all too willingly suspend their disbelief and escape into a fantasy in which eating animals is vegetarianism and endless death is endless life.

Having It *All* in Real Life

The idea that women can have it all has already passed into myth by compressing the components of "all" into the lives of exceptional individuals, all at once. In that mode, many young women are now vicariously having it all, although it is likely that the nature of what they are identifying with owes its magnetic cathexsis for them to an underlying fear that they might not have anything. In reality, in the United States, women still lack universal child care, not to mention universal health care. Those who work outside their homes—the majority—still take on a second shift in domestic and family work. Women are disproportionately subject to domestic violence as well as violence by acquaintances and strangers. Half of all marriages end in divorce, and economic hard times will doubtless intensify the feminization of poverty.

But also in reality, women now live much richer and longer lives than they ever did, and their potential remains untapped. Over the course of their long lives, they may indeed come to have it all, and more, but at different times. For example, if they choose to have children and significant careers, the intensity brought to each of these projects might vary over the decades of a much longer mortal life than enjoyed by poor Bella, who feels pressured to marry, die, and become a vampire herself before she is nineteen, so that she will not look too much older than Edward, who will be seventeen for eternity.

NOTES

1. The box office numbers are available at www.boxofficemojo.com/news/?id=2526&p=s.htm.

2. See Flickr.com, flickr.com/photos/19658365@N00/2831152708.

3. Richard Rorty, "Universality and Truth," in Robert B. Brandom, ed., *Rorty and His Critics* (Oxford, UK: Blackwell, 2000), pp. 21–22.

VAMPIRE LOVE:
THE SECOND SEX
NEGOTIATES THE
TWENTY-FIRST CENTURY

Bonnie Mann

This chapter started in a moment of parental panic. My thirteen-year-old daughter, who habitually reads very thick books of dubious character, was unusually insistent in her pleas to be allowed to attend the midnight release party for the last volume in some book series she was reading. Remembering to thank my lucky stars for her literary commitments, I grudgingly drove her to Borders at about 10 P.M., expecting to see ten or twelve bookish adolescents drinking hot chocolate while they waited for the clock to strike midnight.

The crowded parking lot was my first indication that I was walking into a world everyone knew about, except me. My second was the store, packed wall–to-wall with teenage girls in the full bloom of an almost frighteningly incandescent excitement, many of them dressed in low-cut black gowns with their faces shining like floodlights through pale white paint. I stopped in the doorway of the store and turned to Dee Dee, whose normally beautiful human eyes were already radiating the luminescence of another sphere. I grabbed her arm and held her back. "Just what is this book about?" I asked.

What she gave me to understand with the twenty-five or so words I got out of her before she pulled away was that the glowing faces and the black gowns had something to do with the possibility of being loved by a bloodsucking man.

I later learned that I had delivered my daughter to the release party for *Breaking Dawn*, the fourth and final book of the blockbuster *Twilight* series, by Mormon housewife turned literary millionaire, Stephenie Meyer. These stories, of an all-consuming romance between a human teenage girl named Bella and a vampire frozen in time named Edward, have sold over forty million copies worldwide, and have been translated into thirty-seven languages.

I had to accept that, in the words our new president used to acknowledge Sarah Palin on the campaign trail, vampire love was a "phenomenon." What did it mean that millions of girls were fantasizing about men who could barely repress the desire to kill them? In 2008?

Back in Time

When I opened the first novel, *Twilight*, my impression was that I had gone back in time. The female protagonist struck me as a representative of the idealized womanhood of my mother's generation, transposed into twenty-first-century circumstances. A child of divorced parents, the seventeen-year-old Bella Swan has chosen to go live with her father in the small town of Forks, Washington, on the Olympic Peninsula, leaving Phoenix, Arizona, to give her mother a chance to spend time with her new husband.

Bella loves Phoenix and hates Forks, but self-sacrifice is her specialty. In fact, other than her penchant for self-sacrifice and the capacity to attract the attention of boys, Bella isn't really anyone special. She has no identifiable interests or talents; she is incompetent in the face of almost every challenge. She is the locus of exaggerated stereotypically feminine incapacities and self-loathing. She has no sense of direction or balance. She is prone to get bruises and scrapes just in the process of moving from one place to another and doesn't even trust herself to explore a tide pool without falling in.[1] When she needs something done, especially something mechanical, she finds a boy to do it for her and watches him. Her only areas of skill are cooking and doing laundry, which she does without complaint for her father, who is incompetent in the kitchen in spite of years of living alone (he must have been near starvation when she showed up).

When Bella draws the attention of the stunningly handsome and hyperbolically capable vampire, Edward Cullen, her response is disbelief. "I couldn't imagine anything about me that could be in any way interesting to him," she reports.[2] Frankly, having the feeling that I'd met Bella somewhere before and quickly forgotten the encounter, I couldn't either. When Bella falls in love, then, a girl in love is all she is. By page 139 she has concluded that her mundane life is a small price to pay for the gift of being with Edward, and by the second book she's willing to trade her soul for the privilege.

Edward, in contrast to Bella, is masculine grandiosity writ large. Beautiful beyond compare, the rock-hard seventeen-year-old body Bella comes to worship belongs to a hundred-year-old vampire (frozen in time after a bout with the Spanish flu). He knows everything, having had a hundred years to learn it. He's been everywhere and speaks multiple languages. He reads most people's minds and is strong enough to break a mature tree in two like a matchstick. He runs as fast as most cars drive and rescues the accident-prone Bella over and over; in a first early encounter he rescues her from a vehicle sliding toward her on ice by stopping it with his hands.[3] He is smug and confident and tortured by his desire to drink Bella's blood. He belongs to a cobbled together "family" of vampires who have sworn off human blood for ethical reasons and regularly suck the life out of large game animals instead. Edward's moral struggle with his instinctual bloodlust charges his physically intimate encounters with Bella with erotic, mortal, *and* moral danger. Chivalrous to a fault, he is as deeply concerned with protecting Bella's virtue as he is with keeping her alive.

The strong sense I had of having gone back in time to an old-fashioned world where women were seen as empty conduits of masculine desire and valued for their propensity to self-sacrifice alone drove me to take another look at *The Second Sex* which, widely acknowledged to be a founding text for feminist philosophy, was written by Simone de Beauvoir (1908–1986) half a century ago.[4] De Beauvoir, in contrast to others of the existentialist tradition, never wrote a treatise on the *essence* of love. She asked instead how love is lived and imagined in a *total concrete situation*, by *these* people, at *this* time.

For de Beauvoir in 1949 France, the tragedy of adolescence in the feminine was its demand that the girl give up both herself and her hold on the world. As she enters womanhood, she learns that she is destined to be a "relative being" whose existence has meaning only in relation to the man who loves her. As if Meyer wished to provide the perfect literary illustration of de Beauvoir's claim, when Edward leaves Bella for a time in the second book, Bella describes herself as "like a lost moon—my planet destroyed in some cataclysmic disaster-movie scenario of desolation—that continued . . . to circle in a tight little orbit around the empty space left behind."[5] Bella's mother marvels to her upon seeing her with Edward later in the story, "The way you move—you orient yourself around him without even thinking about it. . . . You're like a . . . satellite."[6]

De Beauvoir claimed that throughout her childhood, the girl learns that "the world is defined without reference to her." [7] Men make history, fight the wars, and produce the great works of art. This lesson becomes a crisis for the adolescent. "To feel oneself passive and dependent at the age of hope and ambition," de Beauvoir wrote, "at the age when the will to live and make a place in the world is running strong. At just this conquering age, woman learns that for her there is to be no conquest, that she must disown herself, that her future depends upon man's good pleasure."[8] What she is offered in exchange for her world-making and value-creating capacities is the love, if she is lucky and pretty enough, of one of the world-makers.

No wonder that the adolescent girl's fantasies of love include a dimension of retreat to the safety of parental protection. After all, the task of becoming a *feminine* adult presents an impossible contradiction. "To be feminine is to appear weak, futile, docile," femininity is a "renunciation of sovereignty,"[9] while adulthood is having the strength and independence to take on the world. This contrast looms large in Meyer's novels. Bella is facing all of the simple cultural markers for adult womanhood: her eighteenth birthday, graduation from high school, first sex, marriage, and motherhood. Yet through most of the story, Bella's vampire is father and mother, as much as lover. By the second book there is a competent, well-muscled werewolf named Jacob who is an equally protective parent. As Bella is handed off for safekeeping from vampire to werewolf and back, she describes the experience as "like when I was a kid and Renée would pass me off to Charlie for the summer."[10] Her weakness contrasted with their strength is that of an infant, contrasted with an all-powerful adult. Edward confides to Bella, "You are so soft, so fragile, I have to mind my actions every moment that we're together so that I don't hurt you. I could kill you very easily Bella, simply by accident . . . you don't realize how incredibly breakable you are."[11] Bella seems to need to be carried everywhere and often falls asleep in the arms of her vampire only to wake up tucked gently into her own bed with him watching over her or playing the lullaby he's written for her; her first dance with Edward is successful because she puts her feet on his and he moves her about the floor.[12] De Beauvoir noted that the woman in love is "trying to reconstruct a situation, that which she experienced as a little girl, under adult protection."[13]

But Bella's physical incapacities carry other meanings. She is a foreigner in physical space, who seems to look over a high fence into the spheres of action and meaning. According to de Beauvoir, the adolescent girl relinquishes her younger self's dominant mode of bodily being, which the German philosopher Edmund Husserl (1859–1938) described as the "I can," the body as the center of living action and intention. When the young girl internalizes and assumes the masculine gaze, de Beauvoir said, she takes up a perspective on herself as prey. As in the fairy tales, she becomes "an idol," a "fascinating treasure," "a marvelous fetish," sought after by men.[14]

In Meyer's books, Bella continually discovers boys looking at her in various modes of desire. The masculine gaze confers meaning on her otherwise empty existence by giving her a place in the story as the very location through which masculine action instantiates meaning. "Through [her beloved]—whose gaze glorifies her," de Beauvoir wrote, "nothingness becomes fullness of being and being is transmuted into worth."[15] Of course, if ever that spotlight should be removed, her very existence is at stake; "the absence of her lover is always torture, he is an eye, a judge."[16] Indeed, when Edward leaves Bella for much of the second book, she sinks into a kind of living death, and it is only the gaze of a virile werewolf that begins to bring her back to life. Part of the seduction of this vampire story must be that, aside from Edward's absence in *New Moon*, his gaze is simply never averted. In a world that is still extremely heavy-handed in its insistence that a young woman's *primary* worth is derived from her ability to awaken masculine desire, Meyer offers girls the fantasy of a male gaze that is intense, constant, and faithful.

When I saw that what de Beauvoir wrote six decades ago seemed so relevant to Meyer's story, my parental panic became dull depression. For de Beauvoir, however timeless the myth of the "eternal feminine" claims to be, it arises from and points back to a total concrete situation, specific in time and place. Certainly the situation of girls in the United States at the dawn of the twenty-first century couldn't be the same as that of girls in 1949 France![17]

The Second Sex in the Twenty-first Century

Truth be told, the legal and formal barriers to women's equality *have* been eroded. A *New York Times* report from 2006 about "the new gender divide" in education noted that "women now make up 58 percent of those enrolled in two- and four-year colleges and are, over all, the majority in graduate schools and professional schools too. Men get worse grades than women," and "women are walking off with a disproportionate share of the honors degrees."[18]

We are accustomed to thinking of women's subordination as a thing of the past. Yet contemporary philosopher Susan Bordo argues that in a media-saturated culture, as gendered power retreats from law and policy it is even more intensely concentrated on women's bodies and the processes by which they come to think of themselves as persons.[19]

Mary Pipher, the acclaimed psychologist whose account of her experiences as a therapist for adolescent girls, *Reviving*

Ophelia, reached number one on the *New York Times* best-seller list over a decade ago, agrees. "Something dramatic happens to girls in early adolescence . . ." she wrote, "they lose their resiliency and optimism and become less curious and inclined to take risks. They lose their assertive, energetic, and 'tomboyish' personalities and become deferential, self-critical, and depressed. They report great unhappiness with their own bodies."[20] This is particularly disconcerting for feminist mothers, because while "we . . . raised our daughters to be assertive and confident . . . they seemed to be insecure and concerned with their femininity."[21] Our messages of equality and opportunity, she noted, are sent out in a world where they run headlong into the "junk values" of a culture obsessed with a narrow version of female beauty. Being attractive to boys is still the first avenue to existence in the imaginary domain of the American middle school girl. In film and on TV women are overwhelmingly represented as "half-clad and half-witted,"[22] while girls are explicitly advised at home and in school that they can be anything they want to be. Girls negotiate these paradoxes at a time when "they don't have the cognitive, emotional, and social skills" to do so, Piper argued. "They are paralyzed by complicated and contradictory data that they cannot interpret. They struggle to resolve the unresolvable and make sense of the absurd."[23] They are overwhelmed by the effort. Describing her own daughter and her friends, Pipher said that at times "they just seemed wrecked. . . . Many confident, well-adjusted girls were transformed into sad, angry failures."[24]

Writer Lynn Philips confirms that these conflicts are not resolved for most young women just by surviving adolescence. Women in college face "an environment filled with tangled messages."[25] A good woman is both *pleasing* in the traditional sense: passive, pleasant, childlike, and subordinate, bent on self-sacrifice; and *together*, meaning she knows who she is and what she wants sexually and professionally, and goes after it.[26]

What young women learn about male sexuality is equally paradoxical.[27] On the one hand, batterers and rapists are pathological exceptions to normal men. On the other hand, male sexuality in general is dangerous, men's "natural sex drive is inherently compelling and aggressive," and young women should not start what they aren't willing to finish.[28] Even today, young women report losing a sense of their own voices in sexual encounters. They feel "a sense of responsibility to go along with and even fake being excited by whatever a male partner [does] in order not to interfere with his arousal."[29]

Young women are presented with two messages about heterosexual love. On the one hand, the notion that love conquers all is ubiquitous—it is presented as a young woman's only chance at salvation. On the other hand is the notion that love hurts, that women can't expect too much from men, who after all are from Mars, not from Venus.[30]

From these contemporary thinkers we learn that while legal inequality has receded, the infantilization of women as objects of male desire has intensified. As subordination has unraveled in arenas of the public sphere, it has retained its hold on the private sphere, especially that most private sphere where the process of becoming who we are is under way. Cultural messages about womanhood are fraught with paradox. And the imaginary domain in which young women negotiate these realities has become a messy place indeed.

A Feminist Subtext

Stephenie Meyer's genius is to clean up that imaginary domain and give girls a story that seems to hold all the contradictions together. While I've already said a great deal about the ways in which Bella seems to be committed to the womanhood we might associate with the 1950s, I haven't said much about the ways that she departs from that representation.

The most surprising thing about Bella's romance with Edward is not that Edward has to resist the urge to perforate her pulsing jugular vein, but that he, not she, puts the brakes on their erotic encounters. Knowing that any loss of control spells death for his beloved, Edward's restraint allows Bella to be the one consumed by desire. She is regularly physically rebuffed by him as she longs to tear off his clothes. In the end, he is pushed into agreeing to sex while she is still human, only by forcing Bella to agree to marry him. We learn that Bella has been "raised to cringe at the very thought of poofy white dresses and bouquets" by her mother, since "early marriage was higher on her blacklist than boiling live puppies."[31] Yet in the end, Bella turns eighteen, graduates, marries Edward for sex, and gets pregnant, practically all at once.

In Phillips's interviews with young women in college, she noted that what was missing from the stew of discourses about sex, love, and sexuality were stories of male accountability and female pleasure without penalty. Meyer offers her readers the first of these missing narratives, which must be a great pleasure for girls who have, no doubt, wished for such stories. As one adolescent girl said to me recently, following an unpleasant encounter with a teenage boy in a car, "I wish he would just get it." Edward gets it. He knows that sex is dangerous for Bella; he reads every sign of emotional distress or joy with extraordinary accuracy and sensitivity.

Meyer still doesn't offer her young readers a clear story of female desire without penalty. For a moment she seems to be providing us with the most brutal critique of heterosexual pleasure and motherhood that we've seen in thirty years. First sex with the vampire leaves the bed in splinters and Bella covered with bruises. She becomes pregnant with a vampire child who threatens destruction from the inside; every fetal kick causes internal bleeding. Depleted to the point of death by the accelerated pregnancy, on the verge of becoming a "broken, bled-out, mangled corpse," Bella drinks human blood, supplied from the blood bank by Edward's doctor vampire father, because nothing else seems to quiet "the little executioner."[32] Rather than letting the little beast chew its way out, a vampire cesarean is performed as Bella plummets toward death; Edward is compelled to inject his venom into Bella to save her, transforming her.

While it took a long time for me to notice, because it is deeply buried, particularly in the first two books, there is a subtle feminist subtext to this vampire love quartet. Bella announces in *Twilight* that she "doesn't like double standards," and writes an essay for her English class on "whether Shakespeare's treatment of the female characters is misogynistic," a subtle textual invitation to the reader to wonder the same thing about Meyer's characters.[33] We discover that Bella wants to be a vampire, not only to avoid out-aging Edward and live with him in immortal bliss, but because in the vampire world, all bets are off when it comes to gender. Vampire women show no particular deference to men. They are endowed with superpowers just like the guys. Rosalie, Edward's vampire sister, is the best mechanic in the family. The female vampires are clearly the answer to the helpless Bella's lament at the end of *Twilight*. "A man and a woman have to be somewhat equal," she says, "as in, one of them can't always be swooping in and saving the other one. They have to save each other equally. . . . I can't always be Lois Lane," she continues, "I want to be Superman too."[34] For the reader, too, the boredom inspired by the thousandth rescue incites hope for something else. "I want to be fierce and deadly," Bella tells us.[35] "Just wait 'til I'm a vampire! I'm not going to be sitting on the sidelines next time."[36]

And though Bella's transformation is a trial by fire (almost literally, since the pain involved in becoming a vampire burns), it does not disappoint. Bella steps back into her "I can" body with a vengeance. "The instant I considered standing erect," she marvels, "I was already straight. There was no brief fragment in time in which the action occurred."[37] She is faster and stronger than Edward. "I could feel it now—the raw, massive strength filling my limbs. I was suddenly sure that if I wanted to tunnel under the river, to claw or beat my way through the bedrock, it wouldn't take me very long."[38] Instead of being carried through the woods by Edward like a baby, she runs with him, "I flew with him through the living green web, by his side, not following at all. . . . I kept waiting to feel winded, but my breath came effortlessly. I waited for the burn to begin in my muscles, but my strength only seemed to increase as I grew accustomed to my stride. My leaping bounds stretched longer, and soon he was trying to keep up with me. I laughed again, exultant, when I heard him falling behind."[39] More than anything, this physical prowess signals an existential change: "Now I was in the story with him," Bella says triumphantly, and the readers, too, sigh with relief.[40] In the final horrific encounter, between good and evil, life and death, it will be Bella, not the boys, who saves the day.

The Price of Existence

What is heartening about Bella is that her story doesn't end the way the fairy tales do, with the kiss that brings the princess back to life, or the wedding at the palace. The fairy-tale ending turns to a nightmare in fact, as the half-vampire fetus beats away at her life. But finally, a self-destructive love bleeds its way into the kind of love de Beauvoir would have described as authentic, a love between two liberties, lived in equality. The tragedy of feminine self-alienation is overcome by journeying *through* it. Meyer sorts the paradoxical narratives of female passivity and power, purity and desire, innocence and responsibility, dependence and autonomy, into a story where one leads, finally, to the other.

When faced with an adult life as what de Beauvoir called "a relative being," a girl may well become convinced that "there is no other way out for her than to lose herself, body and soul, in him who is represented to her as the absolute, the essential."[41] But the ecstasy of this process of self-loss is not, at bottom, masochistic: "She chooses to desire her enslavement so ardently that it appears as the expression of her liberty; she will try to rise above her situation as inessential object by radically assuming it."[42] Under her paroxysm of sacrifice, what de Beauvoir calls the "dream of annihilation," "is in fact an avid will to exist. . . . When woman gives herself to her idol, she hopes that he will give her at once possession of herself and of the universe he represents."[43]

What is disheartening about Meyer's books is her reinstatement of this old promise: assume your status as prey, as object, and you will gain your freedom as subject, as the center of action and meaning. Seek your existence in the eyes of a sovereign masculine subject, and you will find it. The old stories drop the female heroine into an abyss. We don't know what happens to Sleeping Beauty or Cinderella or Snow White after the kiss or the proposal or the wedding—the "happiness" they find is a blank death. But we *do* know what happens to Bella, she is literally torn to shreds by the needs and desires of others. Meyer promises resurrection as a full participant in the not-quite-human drama, and a grasp on the world that is strong—and one imagines Meyer herself, resurrecting herself, furiously writing herself back into existence.

There is a slippage between the promise to the reader and the activity of the writer here. Meyer doesn't come to celebrity life out of the purgatory of feminine nonexistence by letting the blood be drained out of her. It takes a hard-working self-authored creative act to resurrect a woman's life. But how does one open the door of the feminine imagination for young women so that they might trace paths to themselves that don't pass through traditional feminine annihilation? Is the only way to do this through the use of our traditional misogynistic metaphors? If so, Meyer is to be congratulated. But in her insistence on resurrecting the promise that a meaningful life comes *through* self-annihilation in the interests of others, comes *through* appending oneself to one of the special creatures who lives the adventure of life firsthand, she promises our daughters the same things our mothers were promised. In that sense, the wild success of *Twilight* might be cause for despair.

NOTES

1. Stephenie Meyer, *Twilight* (New York: Little, Brown and Company, 2005), p. 116.

2. *Twilight*, p. 228.

3. Ibid., p. 157.

4. Simone de Beauvoir, *The Second Sex*, trans. and ed. by H. M. Parshley (New York: Vintage Books, 1989).

5. Stephenie Meyer, *New Moon* (New York: Little, Brown and Company, 2006), p. 201.

6. Stephenie Meyer, *Eclipse* (New York: Little, Brown and Company, 2007), p. 68.

7. De Beauvoir, *The Second Sex*, p. 331.

8. Ibid., p. 359.

9. Ibid., p. 336.

10. *Eclipse*, p. 236.

11. *Twilight*, p. 310.

12. Ibid., p. 488.

13. De Beauvoir, *The Second Sex*, p. 645.

14. Ibid., p. 350.

15. Ibid., p. 649.

16. Ibid., p. 657.

17. That was just five years after women won the vote there, just seven years after the last person was executed for performing abortions, sixteen years before women could accept paid work without authorization from their husbands, and before the dramatic mobilizations of the 1970s' women's movement.

18. Tamar Lewin, "The New Gender Divide: At Colleges, Women are Leaving Men in the Dust," *New York Times*, July 9, 2006.

19. Several texts make this claim both explicitly and implicity. See *Unbearable Weight: Feminism, Western Culture, and the Body* (Berkeley: University of California Press, 1993); *Twilight Zones: The Hidden Life of Cultural Images from Plato to O.J.* (Berkeley: University of California Press, 1997); *The Male Body: A Look at Men in Public and Private* (New York: Farrar, Straus and Giroux, 1999).

20. Mary Pipher, *Reviving Ophelia: Saving the Selves of Adolescent Girls* (New York: Riverhead Books, 1994), p. 19.

21. Ibid., p. 15.

22. Ibid., p. 42.

23. Ibid., p. 43.

24. Ibid., p. 11.

25. Lynn M. Philips, *Flirting with Danger: Young Women's Reflections on Sexuality and Domination* (New York and London: New York University Press, 2000), p. 18.

26. Ibid., pp. 38–52.

27. Ibid., pp. 52–61.

28. Ibid., p. 58.

29. Ibid., p. 109.

30. Ibid., pp. 69–76.

31. Stephenie Meyer, *Breaking Dawn* (New York: Little, Brown and Company, 2008), pp. 6, 17.

32. Ibid., pp. 355, 357.

33. *Twilight*, pp. 90, 143.

34. Ibid., pp. 473–474.

35. *New Moon*, p. 263.

36. *Eclipse*, p. 559.

37. Ibid., p. 391.

38. Ibid., p. 410.

39. Ibid., p. 413.

40. Ibid., p. 479.

41. De Beauvoir, *The Second Sex*, p. 643.

42. Ibid., p. 643, translation modified by the author.

43. Ibid., p. 646.

EDWARD CULLEN AND BELLA SWAN: BYRONIC AND FEMINIST HEROES . . . OR NOT

Abigail E. Myers

Tall. Pale. Handsome. Mysterious. All of these adjectives describe Edward Cullen from *Twilight*, but these descriptives also classify the traditional Byronic hero within the literary canon. Stephenie Meyer, who earned a B.A. in English from Brigham Young University, named Edward after the characters of Edward Ferrars in Jane Austen's (1775–1817) *Sense and Sensibility* and Edward Rochester in Charlotte Brontë's (1816–1855) *Jane Eyre*—both Byronic heroes. Rochester from *Jane Eyre* particularly provides an interesting parallel to the character of Edward.

Rochester has long been understood as a Byronic hero, an archetype first crafted by British poet George Gordon, Lord Byron (1788–1824).[1] Lord Byron lived the early-nineteenth-century version of the personae he created in literary works such as *Don Juan* (1818) and *Childe Harold's Pilgrimage* (1824). Is Edward Cullen also a Byronic hero? And if he is, what do Jane Eyre's reactions to her Edward teach us about Bella? The answers to these questions give insights into both characters, placing them in their respective literary traditions. Is Meyer attempting to recreate a Byronic hero for twenty-first-century audiences? Let's find out.

You're Only Young Once, but You Can Be Byronic Forever

The Byronic hero is defined by the *Oxford Dictionary of Literary Terms* as a "boldly defiant but bitterly self-tormenting outcast, proudly contemptuous of social norms but suffering for some unnamed sin."[2] He's intelligent, passionate, and usually above-average in almost every way (including good looks), but also tormented, mysterious, unpredictable, and scornful of authority. In other words, he's a "bad boy," the kind of guy your mom warns you about. Or, in our case, would have warned you about if she weren't so busy chasing minor-league ballplayers. But never mind.

Lord Byron, described as "a complex man, and fond of describing his own complexity," had a personality that tended to overshadow his accomplishments as an artist.[3] Getting a literary term named after you usually indicates that you were fairly innovative in your field, and his epic poems are universally considered to be classics of the form. Byron was a rebel known for his prowess as a lover, his adoration of lavish parties and beautiful women, and his somewhat bizarre decision at the end of his life to join the Greek War of Independence. But if you like that kind of thing, *Childe Harold's Pilgrimage* is most often cited as the chief example of Byron's eponymous hero, and it's not hard to see why, given these lines from the poem:

Whilome in Albion's isle there dwelt a youth
Who ne in Virtue's ways did take delight,
But spent his days in riot most uncouth,
And vexed with mirth the drowsy ear of Night.
Ah me! In sooth he was a shameless wight,
Sore given to revel and ungodly glee,
Few earthly things found favor in his sight
Save concubines and carnal companie,
And flaunting wassailers of high and low degree.

. . .

Yet oftimes in his maddest mirthful mood
Strange pangs would flash along Childe Harold's brow,
As if the Memory of some deadly feud
Or disappointed passion lurked below:
But this none knew, nor haply cared to know;
For his was not that open, artless soul
That feels relief by bidding sorrow flow;
Nor sought he friend to counsel or condole,
Whate'er this grief mote be, which he could not control.[4]

Hmm. Does that sound like anyone we know? Someone who likes to cause trouble at night and drive fast cars has self-control issues and some "deadly feuds"? The poem could easily be describing Meyer's Edward Cullen, though it was written 180 years before *Twilight* ever hit bookshelves. There is an implied immortality to the figure of the Byronic hero; Meyer's use of Byronic characteristics for Edward, immortal as both a vampire and a Byronic hero, show a deeper level of meaning to the book series that has swept the tween population in the United States.

Why Byronic Heroes Make Bad Bosses

Edward Rochester. The name alone evokes sighs from generations of readers of the immortal *Jane Eyre*, by Charlotte

Brontë, first published in 1847 under the pseudonym Currer Bell. The story of a poor but passionate governess who falls in love with her dark, mysterious, tormented employer (are we seeing a pattern here yet?), *Jane Eyre* is a hallmark of British Victorian literature that has inspired movies, graphic novels, and contemporary romances for nearly two hundred years.[5] Why is Edward Rochester a Byronic hero so worth imitating? You should read the book, but in case you just can't get out of line for the *New Moon* premiere long enough to run over to a bookstore, let's take a look.[6]

Jane, who narrates the book, attends a school for orphaned girls and is, upon leaving, hired by an elderly housekeeper to be the governess to a single child, Adele, at the magnificent manor of Thornfield. (Note: Bookish young lady starts a new life far from home, with no friends and a sense of both adventure and trepidation. Sound familiar?) The master, she is told, is home infrequently, and she spends most of her time with Adele and the household help. She meets Edward Rochester, Adele's father and the man who owns Thornfield, after he has a riding mishap while Jane is out for a walk. Almost immediately she finds herself confused by and attracted to Rochester: "[H]e looked preciously grim, cushioning his massive head against the swelling back of his chair, and receiving the light of the fire on his granite-hewn features, and in his great, dark eyes, and very fine eyes, too—not without a certain change in their depths sometimes, which, if it were not softness, reminded you, at least, of that feeling."[7]

But wasting no time, Edward Rochester also cautions Jane about himself:

> I am a trite common-place sinner, hackneyed in all the poor petty dissipations with which the rich and worthless try to put on life. . . . I could reform—I have strength yet for that—if—but where is the use of

thinking of it, hampered, burdened, cursed as I am? Besides, since happiness is irrevocably denied me, I have a right to get pleasure out of life: and I *will* get it, cost what it may.[8]

Of course, this little speech sets Jane's heart a-fluttering, and eventually our hero and heroine declaim their undying love for each other. Here's the problem: Jane is a good girl and Rochester is a bad boy. *A very bad boy.* Without spoiling the story for those of you camping outside the multiplex, Jane eventually discovers Rochester's nasty little secret (every good Byronic hero has at least one), and tells him, in no uncertain Victorian terms, to shove it.[9] She wants him to get the message so badly that she lights out from Thornfield with just about nothing and no plan beyond seeing how far a carriage will take her on the little bit of money she has. She leaves Thornfield before sunrise with this thought: "[He] was waiting with impatience for day. He would send for me in the morning; I should be gone. He would have me sought for: vainly. He would feel himself forsaken; his love rejected: he would suffer; perhaps grow desperate. I thought of this too. My hand moved towards the lock: I caught it back, and glided on."[10]

Cold, huh? What kind of sweet, innocent girl is Jane anyway to run off like that? Aren't nice girls supposed to stand by their man, longing for them à la Bella Swan in *New Moon*? Not this girl.

Jane Eyre: Gritty Governess, Runaway Bride, and Feminist Hero

Sandra M. Gilbert's and Susan Gubar's introduction to *Jane Eyre* says that in the book "a determined female narrator spoke with what was in 1847 surprising authority about a woman's desire for liberty."[11] Indeed, Jane herself has long been understood as a revolutionary character in literature, a game-changer, a prototype for the sort of hero we would call "feminist" today. Or would we?

Jane works as a governess after leaving a strict, conservative girls' school, a fairly typical feminine occupation during the nineteenth century. Her narrative meets a rather conventional ending for women in 1847. She is accomplished in the genteel arts of women—drawing, playing piano, sewing, and the like. When contemporary readers imagine feminist heroes, we might imagine Agent Scully, Hermione Granger, President Laura Roslin, even Bridget Jones or Carrie Bradshaw, but probably not a nineteenth-century governess. Today, we want our feminist heroes to be tough, gun-packing, no-nonsense types or even career women with shoe and weight obsessions, but probably not a prim, perfectly collected young woman for whom a bonnet was a must-have.

But we'd be wrong. Jane can be understood as a feminist character for her determination to stick to her moral guns (no matter what nonsense some man tries to sell her), her belief in her ethics and academic education, her ability and willingness to support herself, and her loyalty to her friends. For example, when Edward Rochester tries talking Jane into staying with him despite her knowledge of his terrible secret, she refuses. If only Bella were as wise. Jane knows that staying with Rochester would mean compromising her deeply held principles of morality, though she also knows that she will find it difficult to leave the man she has come to love:

> I care for myself. The more solitary, the more friendless, the more unsustained I am, the more I will respect myself. I will keep the law given by God; sanctioned by man. I will hold to the principles received by me. . . . Laws and principles are not for times when there is no temptation: they are for such moments as this, when body and soul rise in mutiny against their rigour; stringent are they; inviolate they shall be. If at

my individual convenience I might break them, what would be their worth? They have a worth—so I have always believed.[12]

As well, when Jane finds that she must start over with nothing, she calmly prepares to use whatever experience and education she possesses to support herself. "Yes, very," she says, when asked if she is "book-learned"; "I was at board-ing-school eight years."[13] But when asked what kind of work she can do, she says, "Show me how to work, or how to seek work: that is all I now ask; then let me go . . . I will be a dressmaker: I will be a plain work-woman; I will be a servant, a nurse-girl, if I can be no better."[14] When she is offered a position as a teacher at a small country school for girls, she comments, "In truth it was humble—but then it was sheltered, and I wanted a safe asylum: it was plodding—but then, compared with that of a governess in a rich house, it was independent; and the fear of servitude with strangers entered my soul like iron: it was not ignoble—not unwor-thy—not mentally degrading."[15] These statements show that while Jane is proud of her education, her foremost goal is to be self-supporting and independent. Bella shares some of these qualities as well, like not wanting Charlie, her father, to purchase a car for her when she first arrives in Forks, and flying to Washington on her own to live with Charlie and then back to Arizona when being pursued by James. Even her interest in Edward suggests Bella's intent on becoming inde-pendent, if not self-supported.

Finally, like all feminist heroes worth their salt, Jane Eyre is intensely loyal to her friends, as is Bella (Jacob—need I say more?). When Jane is shocked by the news that she has inher-ited a large fortune from an uncle she has never met, she is far more excited by the information that the Rivers family, with whom she lived after fleeing Thornfield, is also related to her. She chooses to share the fortune with the other members of the family, despite their insistence that she keep the money for herself: "I could not forego the delicious pleasure of which I have caught a glimpse—that of repaying, in part, a mighty obligation, and winning to myself life-long friends. . . . [Y]ou . . . cannot at all imagine the craving I have for fraternal and sisterly love. I never had a home, I never had brothers or sisters; I must and will have them now."[16]

So, while Jane's most formidable weapon might be her drawing pencils with an educational equivalent to today's ninth or tenth grade, it's not hard to see why critics and readers have understood her as a feminist hero, a fascinating and unusual foil for the Byronic bad boy of Edward Rochester. Though he considers the vacuous and spoiled belles of the various balls like Blanche Ingram, the modest yet self-possessed, strong-willed Jane wins his heart. Nice girls finish first in all conceivable ways in *Jane Eyre*, gaining material wealth, familial connections, romantic love, as well as moral and intellectual satisfaction.

But what does it all have to do with the *Twilight* saga? You've seen the superficial parallels to Edward and Bella. Let's see how those two crazy kids from Forks really measure up to these timeless characters.

The Byronic Hero: Now Available in Marble-like, Sparkly Perfection

Edward becomes Bella's love interest fairly early in *Twilight*. It's pretty hard to miss that dude who broods but never eats in the high school cafeteria with his extremely attractive family, driving a sports car to school when most of the other boys have pickup trucks with gun racks. Does he fit the mold of the Byronic hero? Well, do vampires drink blood?

We learned earlier in this chapter that Byronic heroes are not without their good qualities. They're usually smart, and Edward flashes his knowledge of biology early on in his and Bella's initial pairing as lab partners.[17] Byronic heroes are brave, as Edward shows when he saves Bella from the car crash.[18] And when a Byronic hero decides to focus his interest on something, he is passionate, as Edward admits to Bella:

[Bella:] "Why didn't you want to leave?"

[Edward:] "It makes me . . . anxious . . . to be away from you." His eyes were gentle but intense, and they seemed to be making my bones turn soft.[19] "I wasn't joking when I asked you to try not to fall in the ocean or get run over last Thursday. I was distracted all weekend, worrying about you."[20]

But Byronic heroes are dangerous, too—so dangerous that they like to *come right out and tell you how dangerous they are.* Just like Childe Harold and Edward Rochester! They do not hide how messed up they are; they revel in it, talk about it, write about it, sparkle in a field about it. Edward Cullen certainly fits in here: "'Don't you see, Bella? It's one thing for me to make myself miserable, but a wholly other thing for you to be so involved.' He turned his anguished eyes to the road, his words flowing almost too fast for me to understand. . . . His voice was low but urgent. His words cut me. 'It's wrong. It's not safe. I'm dangerous, Bella—please, grasp that.'"[21] He totally cribbed that from Edward Rochester.

And since no Byronic hero is without his terrible, dreadful secret, Edward Cullen has a big one: He's a century-old vampire. He unburdens himself of his secret somewhat earlier than Rochester, and you have to give Bella props for figuring it out long before Jane Eyre did:

"I did some research on the Internet."

"And did that convince you?" His voice sounded barely interested. But his hands were clamped hard onto the steering wheel.

"No. [. . .] I decided it didn't matter," I whispered.

"It didn't *matter*?" His tone made me look up—I had finally broken through his carefully composed mask. His face was incredulous, with just a hint of the anger I'd feared.

"No," I said softly. "It doesn't matter to me what you are."

A hard, mocking edge entered his voice. "You don't care if I'm a monster? If I'm not *human*?"[22]

Of course, Edward's secret is softened quite significantly by his "vegetarianism"; he and the rest of the Cullen family live on the blood of animals, obtained during their "hunting" trips in the forests surrounding Forks. But that doesn't mean that he and his vampire family have totally lost their interest in human blood. Being around humans is a struggle for the whole clan on occasion, except for Carlisle Cullen, the "father" and the most superbly self-controlled of the veggie vampires, as he explains when Bella cuts herself at her birthday party in *New Moon*.[23]

Bella is the biggest challenge of all for Edward. Though he wants to protect her and love her in a human way, his desire for her blood (and, by extension, her death as a human and eventual transformation into a vampire herself) never goes away. He explains to Bella in chapter 14 of *Twilight*, titled appropriately enough "Mind Over Matter," how he teaches himself control around her so that they can enjoy something that resembles a typical human relationship.[24] But the Byronic hero is always fighting his past, figuratively and literally, a flaw that shows itself most stunningly in *Twilight* when Edward takes on the decidedly-not-vegetarian vampire crew of James, Laurent, and Victoria, and dispatches James, Victoria's partner, to be finished off by his "brothers," Emmett and Jasper.[25] Edward may be the picture of gentlemanly restraint around the all-too-human Bella, but his superhuman strength and ruthless efficiency as a killer reveal themselves to Bella with crystalline clarity by the end of *Twilight*.

So clearly we have a somewhat flawed (to say the least) hero in Edward without even getting into his control-freak tendencies where Bella is concerned.[26] But what of Bella, the intrepid lover of vampires and eventual vampire-wife-and-mama herself? Is she a feminist hero in the tradition of the imitated-but-never-replicated Jane Eyre? Well, let's examine the evidence.

Can You Still Be a Feminist If You Become a Bloodsucking Vampire for Your Husband?

Bella is a puzzle for feminists. On one hand, we have a hero who is literate, is independent, and goes after what she wants, just like our friend Jane. She reads *Wuthering Heights*! She hauls off to the middle of sweet nowhere alone despite the love of a kind, if somewhat flaky, mother. And despite the many good reasons for not getting involved, she remains devoted to Edward to the point of going under the fang and transforming into a beautiful and fearsome vampire. These seem like reasonable arguments for Bella being a fierce and fabulous feminist hero, a model of steely determination, stolid independence, and undying passion for young women of the iPod generation.

But critics, bloggers, fans, and this author have a lot to say about Bella's suitability as a feminist role model for the millions of teenage girls (and, let's be honest, adult women) who have picked up the saga. One of the most cogent (and hilarious) is blogger Cleolinda Jones, whose retellings of and commentaries on the saga have received thousands of hits in just under a year. For example, in *New Moon*, Bella begins to spend time with Jacob Black after Edward's disappearance, an event that makes her morose and eventually suicidal. When Jacob shows off some motorcycles they plan to restore (unbeknownst to Jacob, so Bella can attempt suicide-by-Harley), Bella comments, "I figured I'd have to have a Y chromosome to really understand the excitement."[27] Jones responds, "Because *girrrrrlllllls* [*sic*] can't enjoy awesome things like motorcycles. Unless they're trying to kill themselves."[28]

This pithy observation highlights the central conflict with Bella and feminism: Edward eventually becomes the only raison d'être for Bella. She seems to have few interests or passions outside of Edward. The kindness and affection shown to her by Jacob are cast aside when Edward returns at the end of *New Moon*.[29] Her friendships with some of the girls at school are superficial and easily forgotten; only two of her friends from school are guests at her wedding in *Breaking Dawn*, and we never see them again after that. Even her relationship with her well-intentioned and loving, if not awkward, father, is a casualty of her relationship with Edward. Unlike Jane Eyre, Bella does not share the spoils of fortune with her friends and family; Edward becomes all that matters.

Most troubling, Bella unquestioningly accepts all of Edward's worst qualities. Sure, there's not much he can do about being a vampire, and he does control himself pretty admirably in that department. But, as Jones and others have commented, Edward's attention to Bella mirrors disturbingly a relationship that would be called abusive in the real world. His sneaking into her bedroom at night to watch her sleep—initially, unbeknownst to her—is the kind of thing that would make most of us call the cops and report a stalker, if we didn't whack him with the Louisville Slugger next to the bed first. He doesn't encourage her to pursue other friendships or interests outside of him (indeed, he is intensely jealous of even conversations she has with other boys), apart from his vague warnings that he is "dangerous," and insists on following her and accompanying her almost everywhere. And when Edward eventually confesses the lie that drives most of the plot of *New Moon*, he seems offended that Bella has a hard time believing his story. Jones snarks, "Also, it's kind of pissing me off that Edward's mad that she won't believe him now. 'What? I just told you a gigantic, sadistic lie that rendered you catatonic for six months! Why are you not believing a single word I say *now?*'"[30]

Just like your garden-variety Byronic hero, Bella has her good qualities; but, again like the Byronic hero, she's not necessarily someone you'd want your kid to emulate or fall in love with. It's hard to compare Bella with Jane Eyre and still find Bella to be a feminist hero; if any character from that time period comes to mind when discussing Bella it is Cathy Earnshaw, the destructive antagonist in Emily Brontë's (yes, that would be Charlotte's sister) *Wuthering Heights*. Is it any wonder that *Wuthering Heights*, rather than *Jane Eyre*, is Bella's favorite book by a Brontë sister?

Self-Exiled Harold Wanders Forth Again; or, Basically, Bella and Edward Deserve Each Other

The key difference between Edward Rochester and Edward Cullen is that Rochester learns his lesson. Because Jane has ovaries enough to show him that she won't put up with his crap—and backs up her statements with a predawn escape that confounds him and breaks his heart—Edward Rochester truly understands how selfish and short-sighted he is. He also goes through an unbelievable punishment that involves death, destruction, and disability, directly caused by his lack of understanding, compassion, and foresight.[31] She only returns to him when the circumstance that caused her to leave in the first place is resolved and she has proof that he truly reformed. It is her faith, her education, and her self-reliance (and, okay, a convenient inheritance that would make her a modern-day "Real Housewife of Northern England") that allows her to support herself without Edward and also allow her to have a relationship with him based on equality and mutual respect.

Bella, on the other hand—well, not so much. A feminist response to Edward Cullen might have been, "Look, you seem like a really nice vampire, but if being with you means giving up my family, my friends, and my hopes for higher education, I think I'm going to seek out a relationship that allows me to have romantic and sexual love as well as all that other stuff." And a nonabusive vampire would have really meant it when he said that the beautiful mortal girl was better off without him, and would have allowed that being mortal, human, and young includes making your own mistakes and *not* being insulated from every possible threat, real or imagined.

But that doesn't cross Bella and Edward's minds. The ending they find is truly a fairy tale, not because it seems happily ever after but because it lacks cause and effect, moral responsibility, and real relationships. And if that's Stephenie Meyer's idea of a fairy-tale ending, maybe we'd all better make sure that we take the *Twilight* saga for what it is: a fairy tale, no more worthy of emulation than *Sleeping Beauty*. The test? Ask yourself if Sleeping Beauty is a role model. I'm guessing the answer is no. Well, then, is Bella a feminist hero? Maybe we can answer that with another question: Will vampires ever get over their taste for blood?[32]

NOTES

1. George Gordon became Lord Byron at the age of ten, inheriting the title from his father. He dropped the "Gordon" from his name, generally, after that point, as was the custom of the day. See Frank D. McConnell, ed. *Byron's Poetry* (New York: Norton and Company, 1978).

2. Chris Baldick, *Oxford Dictionary of Literary Terms* (Oxford: Oxford University Press, 2008). *Oxford Reference Online*, Oxford University Press, St. John's University, www.oxfordreference.com/views/ENTRY.html?subview=Main&entry=t56.e155.

3. McConnell, *Byron's Poetry*, p. xi.

4. Ibid., pp. 26–27.

5. For my money, the only film adaptation of *Jane Eyre* worth watching is the BBC's four-part miniseries from 2006. Read about it here: www.bbc.co.uk/drama/janeeyre/about.shtml.

6. An excellent Internet reference on *Jane Eyre* is "Charlotte's Web," easily accessed from your favorite computer at www.umd.umich.edu/casl/hum/eng/classes/434/charweb/index.html.

7. Charlotte Brontë, *Jane Eyre* (New York: Barnes and Noble Books, 1993), p. 131.

8. Ibid., p. 136.

9. Spoiler alert! The secret is that Rochester's first wife is not only alive and still married to him, but insane and locked up in the attic in Thornfield. Jane finds out not during a quiet, rational discussion with her husband-to-be, but—get this—at the "Are there any objections?" part of her wedding ceremony. Now, that's a reason for a woman to turn into a Bridezilla.

10. Brontë, *Jane Eyre*, p. 328.

11. Sandra M. Gilbert and Susan Gubar, eds., *The Norton Anthology of Literature by Women*, 2nd ed. (New York: Norton and Company, 1996).

12. Brontë, *Jane Eyre*, p. 325.

13. Ibid., p. 349.

14. Ibid., pp. 357–358.

15. Ibid., p. 364.

16. Ibid., pp. 397–398.

17. Stephenie Meyer, *Twilight* (New York: Little, Brown and Company, 2005), p. 45.

18. *Twilight*, p. 56.

19. A heretofore unrealized unifying trait of Byronic heroes: intense eyes. I'll take that Genius Grant now, MacArthur Foundation.

20. *Twilight*, pp. 188–189.

21. Ibid., p. 190.

22. Ibid., p.184.

23. Stephenie Meyer, *New Moon* (New York: Little, Brown and Company, 2006), pp. 33–36.

24. *Twilight*, pp. 293–311.

25. Ibid., p. 461.

26. For a fascinating feminist take on Edward's issues in this department, read "I Was a Teenage Trend-Hater: Despising *Twilight* Is Big for Fall," Jezebel.com, jezebel.com/5092089/i-was-a-teenage-trend+hater-despising-twilight-is-big-for-fall.

27. *New Moon*, p. 139.

28. Cleolinda Jones, "Twilight II: Vampiric Boogaloo," *Occupation: Girl*, May 15, 2008, clcolinda.livejournal.com/603861.html.

29. *New Moon*, p. 561.

30. Jones, "Twilight II: Vampiric Boogaloo."

31. Yet another spoiler alert! Rochester's crazy wife eventually commits suicide after setting the fire that burns Thornfield to the ground and blinds Rochester. I'd say that's sufficient punishment for attempting bigamy and then trying to convince a nice gal like Jane to be his mistress.

32. I would like to dedicate this essay to Dr. Laurie Sterling at King's College, without whom I never would have given *Jane Eyre* a second thought after my disastrous attempt at reading it as a fourteen-year-old. Her lucid and passionate teaching of *Jane Eyre* could surely convince even Meyer's teenage audience to pick up this thick but rewarding classic.

twelve

UNDEAD PATRIARCHY AND THE POSSIBILITY OF LOVE

Leah McClimans and J. Jeremy Wisnewski

There are lots of reasons to distrust Edward Cullen when we first meet him. Drinking blood is only one of them. He seems to be a (stereo)typical man in every respect: he has trouble controlling his urges, he's rude, and he always thinks *he* knows best. Even his initial attraction to Bella Swan seems to be marked by a desire for control. Think about it: Edward doesn't have access to Bella's thoughts, so he doesn't immediately have the same advantage over her that he does with others. She thus refuses (albeit unintentionally) to fall under his power. But this fact seems to make her all the more enticing to Edward, a control freak par excellence: since he doesn't automatically have access to her mind, he longs to find out about her—and thereby to master her.

Of course, maybe we're not giving Edward the benefit of the doubt, but can you blame us? Under patriarchy, men don't have the best track record, to put it mildly. A patriarchy is a society, like ours, characterized by structures that support male dominance. Equality in opposite-sex relationships is difficult to achieve. We're socialized to think of human relations in terms of the strong and the weak; winners and losers; protectors and the protected.[1] As a result, when faced with controlling and overbearing behavior from partners and boyfriends, women and girls (including Bella) often interpret that behavior as caring and romantic. Likewise, men and boys (including Edward) often interpret their female counterparts as irrational and silly.[2] Feminists argue that, if unchecked, this lack of equality undermines trust, honesty, and ultimately, love.

These patterns of domination and subordination continue in our society, even though most girls today are raised to become women who see themselves as individuals with an equal social status. Recognizing oneself as an equal *individual*, sadly, is not the same as understanding oneself as an equal member of a heterosexual relationship (or any other relationship, for that matter). And there's little help around for understanding *how* to have an equal relationship. Indeed, we might even wonder, with Andrea Dworkin, whether or not there *can* be equal heterosexual relations.[3] Surprising as it sounds, this lack of guidance is why we need the *Twilight* saga. We need to see Edward learn to be a better person and less of a stereotypical man. In Forks, Washington, we find both the pitfalls of patriarchy and the possibility of a love that recognizes the necessity of equality.

The Control Issues of Edward Cullen

As the story goes, an unknown vampire breaks into Bella's house while she spends the weekend held "hostage" at the Cullens'. The veggie vamps and the local werewolves go on red alert. Jacob Black comes over to the Swans' to get the intruder's scent. On his way out, he decides to ask Bella out:

"Hold up a sec—hey, do you think you can come to La Push tonight? We're having a bonfire party. Emily will be there, and you could meet Kim . . ."

"Yeah, Jake, I don't know about that. See, it's a little tense right now . . ."

"C'mon, you think somebody's going to get past all—all six of us?" . . . His eyes were full of unashamed pleading.

"I'll ask," I said doubtfully.

He made a noise in the back of his throat. "Is he your warden, now too? You know, I saw this story on the news last week about controlling, abusive teenage relationships and—"

"Okay!" I cut him off, and then shoved his arm. "Time for the werewolf to get out!"[4]

Of course, Jacob will say *anything* to press his advantage with Bella, but this time he might be on to something. Edward *can* be very controlling. Feminists for some time have recognized controlling relationships as one consequence of patriarchy. A system that promotes male domination also encourages men to fear the ways in which their domination may be diminished. As a result, men attempt to control situations in which they feel most vulnerable. Bella may not be the most beautiful girl in Forks, but she seems to be the most desirable—and she's Edward's. Not surprisingly, Edward's control issues most often stem from his fear for Bella's safety—just those situations that would take her away from him. When Bella meets the Cullen family for the first time, she notices a silent exchange between Carlisle and Edward. A bit later she asks Edward,

"So what was Carlisle telling you before?"

His eyebrows pulled together. "You noticed that, did you?"

I shrugged. "Of course."

He looked at me thoughtfully for a few seconds before answering. "He wanted to tell me some news—he didn't know if it was something I would share with you."

"Will you?"

"I have to, because I'm going to be a little . . . overbearingly protective over the next few days—or weeks—and I wouldn't want you to think I'm naturally a tyrant."

"What's wrong?"

"Nothing's wrong, exactly. Alice just sees some visitors coming soon. They know we're here, and they're curious."

"Visitors?"

"Yes . . . well, they aren't like us, of course—in their hunting habits, I mean. They probably won't come into town at all, but I'm certainly not going to let you out of my sight till they're gone."[5]

Apparently Bella has no choice in the matter, and Edward intends to "protect" her by controlling where she goes and whom she sees. And it gets worse. Before long, Edward is withholding information from Bella (remember early in *Eclipse* when he lies to Bella about Alice's vision of Victoria's return?), manipulating her (remember that trip to Florida?), tailing her car (scaring her sufficiently that she doesn't want to look at him in the rearview mirror), and paying Alice to hold her hostage while he goes off for a weekend with the boys.

Controlling behavior may be the result of patriarchy, but it also reinforces it. The more Edward feels the need to protect Bella, the more he views her as weak and vulnerable.

Moreover, his view of her is not simply in terms of her physical weakness, but it also applies to his assessment of her decision-making capacity. Perhaps no example illustrates this point as well as Bella's and Edward's ongoing argument about whether she will become a vampire. Edward *continually* dismisses Bella's request as irrational, uninformed, and hasty. Or consider in *New Moon* when Edward decides to leave Bella. He does so *not* because he's tired of pretending to be something he's not, but rather, as he later explains to her, "I only left you in the first place because I wanted you to have a chance at a normal, happy, human life. I could see what I was doing to you—keeping you constantly on the edge of danger, taking you away from the world you belonged in, risking your life every moment I was with you."[6]

Edward's explanation may sound self-sacrificing, but Bella doesn't *want* a "normal, happy, human life," and she didn't *want* Edward to leave. How many times does Bella beg Edward to stay with her? How often does she ask him to change her? In fact, a "normal, happy, human life" increasingly becomes Bella's worst-case scenario. Why does Edward consistently think that he knows better than Bella regarding what is in her best interest? It can't be Bella's track record with decision-making. Bella is an excellent decision-maker: When Bella sees that her mother needs to spend time traveling with her new husband, she decides to move in with her dad—and this turns out to be a good decision. When James begins to track her, it's Bella who decides on their course of action—a much better plan than Edward's strap-her-in-the-Jeep-and-drive-till-morning strategy. And it can't be Bella's lack of maturity. She's incredibly mature: She practically raised herself, she kept her mother out of trouble for seventeen years, and she looks after her domestically challenged father. So what is it? Could it be, just maybe—Edward thinks he knows better than Bella because he's a man?

Bella's Mixed Reactions

Feminists highlight two reactions to this kind of controlling behavior. On the one hand, women and girls resent being controlled and resort to clandestine behavior such as lying, sneaking around, and their own brand of manipulation. On the other hand, they interpret controlling behavior as a sign of care and commitment.

We see both in Bella. Bella rebels against Edward's authority at the same time that she regards it as a sign of his love for her. When Bella first escapes to La Push against Edward's orders, she plans to be at work at Newton's. But when she unexpectedly gets the day off, she puts the pedal to the metal and sneaks off to visit Jacob before Alice can see what she's planning. Yet, a few days later, when Edward has Alice hold Bella hostage and Bella calls Jacob to cancel their upcoming plans, she accepts Edward's behavior as an expression of love.

> "I wish. I'm not at Charlie's," I said sourly. "I'm kind of being held prisoner."
>
> He was silent as that sunk in, and then he growled. "We'll come and get you," he promised in a flat voice, slipping automatically into a plural.
>
> A chill slid down my spine, but I answered in a light and teasing voice. "Tempting. I have been tortured—Alice painted my toenails."
>
> "I'm serious."
>
> "Don't be. They're just trying to keep me safe."
>
> He growled again.
>
> "I know it's silly, but their hearts are in the right place."[7]

Bella is comfortable with lying because she feels the control being used is for her own safety, but she also hints at resentment, though her need to lie to a friend and her resentment of being held "prisoner" both should have been red flags to Bella that her relationship with Edward was not necessarily a healthy one.

Edward's Progress

Patriarchal societies support inequality between men and women: Men are strong and rational; women are weak and silly. For many feminist theorists, controlling behavior is a consequence of patriarchy: Men will try to control those situations in which their dominant status is threatened. Controlling behavior, however, also reinforces systems of domination and subordination, in that the women whom men attempt to control are taken to be in *need* of control—in need of guidance, protection, and oversight. Moreover, the tendency to interpret controlling behavior as romantic and the inclination to escape it by lying and manipulating means that it is often difficult to overcome.

The tragedy is that controlling behavior doesn't signify love; instead, it creates a barrier to it. Control requires both men and women to lie and manipulate their partners, but such behavior is at odds with love because it's an obstacle to respect and trust. For feminist theorist bell hooks, respect and trust are two dimensions of love; to embrace love we must embrace care, commitment, responsibility, trust, respect, and knowledge.[8]

According to hooks, this embrace is possible only if we first break with patriarchy and recognize our partners as equals. Bella and Edward begin this break when Bella questions Edward's motivation for keeping her away from the werewolves:

> The words popped out thoughtlessly. "Is this really just about my safety?"
>
> "What do you mean?" he demanded.
>
> "You aren't . . ." Angela's theory seemed sillier now than before. It was hard to finish the thought. "I mean, you know better than to be jealous right?"

He raised one eyebrow. "Do I?"

"Be serious."

"Easily—there's nothing remotely humorous about this."

I frowned suspiciously. "Or . . . is this something else altogether? Some vampires-and-werewolves-are-always-enemies nonsense? Is this just a testosterone-fueled—"

His eyes blazed. "This is only about you. All I care is that you're safe."[9]

But despite Edward's assurance, a week later he changes his mind. When he returns from his weekend of hunting, he finds out that his plan to have Alice hold Bella hostage was only semisuccessful—Jacob sprung Bella from school on the back of his motorcycle and they spent the day together in La Push. Unlike the other occasions when Bella spent time with Jacob, Edward does not lose his mind. What's different?

"I decided that you were right. My problem before was more about my . . . prejudice against werewolves than anything else. I'm going to try to be more reasonable and trust your judgment. If you say it's safe, then I'll believe you."

"Wow."

"And . . . most importantly . . . I'm not willing to let this drive a wedge between us."[10]

In his decision to trust Bella's judgment, Edward decides to treat her as a person with the ability to make sound decisions; he decides to treat her as an equal. He no longer views Bella as a weak human girl whose decisions are necessarily dubious, but rather sees her as a person whose decisions and rationale must be taken seriously and respected—even when he disagrees with them. Moreover, Edward recognizes that this move toward equality is important in order to preserve their relationship. He recognizes that his attempts to keep her from Jacob—his attempts to control her actions—will only drive her away from him, both literally and figuratively.

Edward's decision to trust Bella's judgment regarding the werewolves is certainly not the end of Edward's controlling behavior. After all, as he tells Bella during their first time in the meadow, he's only human. Structures of dominance are not thrown off in one day or by one decision. But Edward continues increasingly to trust Bella's decisions even though sometimes his progress is not smooth (remember all of their conversations about sex?) and sometimes it's in spite of himself (remember how badly he wants her to have an abortion?). Nonetheless, he gets better. He learns to negotiate with her when they disagree. At the end of *Eclipse*, he finally appreciates how harmful some of his behavior has been: "I've clung with such idiotic obstinacy to my idea of what's best for you, though it's only hurt you. Hurt you so deeply, time and time again. I don't trust myself anymore. You can have happiness your way."[11]

Talked into Love

This emerging equality intensifies Bella and Edward's already intense intimacy. Freed from the need to lie and manipulate each other, they are ever more able to talk honestly about their fears, their expectations, and their desires. Such honesty is the first step in the process of love, as hooks suggests: It signals trust and respect, and thus a break with patriarchy and control.[12] Score one for Bella and Edward.

The second step in the process of love, hooks tells us, is communication.[13] Communication is important because on the one hand, it allows us to experience our significant others as persons like ourselves (people with similar fears, hopes, ambitions), and this experience makes it difficult to participate in a relationship based on dominance and subordination. On the other hand, communication is important because it gives us knowledge of our partners, and this knowledge helps us to know how better to love them.

But despite the importance of communication, we're rarely given examples in the media or in fiction of lovers who communicate with each other. Romantic comedies are not awash in communicative honesty, and even the classics seem to underemphasize how important open communication is to the work of love (we're talking about you, Shakespeare!). Romeo and Juliet have very little to say to each other, except how much they're in love—which is rather amazing, given that they know absolutely nothing about one another. And as far as what makes the headlines? Well, we're too busy fretting over celebrity relationships to ask about the importance of communication in a truly equal and loving relationship; we're more interested in the strange metaphysical morphings of separate persons into monolithic "Bennifers" and "Brangelinas."

Through these examples we're led to believe that it's possible to love someone without really talking to him or her—without really knowing the person at all. We're led to believe that a physical attraction or fate is all we need in order to love. We're even led to believe that knowledge of our partner would make love less compelling, less romantic.

But Bella and Edward have a relationship that acts as antidote to these misconceptions about love and the necessity of communication in fostering it. Their relationship is even *stranger* than your normal vampire-human love tryst because almost all Bella and Edward do is talk, talk, talk. We can learn much about how love develops and endures from their conversations.

Of course, Bella and Edward *are* immediately attracted to each other. For Edward, Bella's appearance in biology changes his definition of the word *thirsty*; and from her first lunch at Forks High, Bella is dazzled by Edward's beauty. But this attraction is only the beginning of their story.

At first Edward wants to kill Bella for her blood, but before long it isn't just her scent that's attractive; Bella intrigues Edward. She doesn't act like other humans: She never tells anyone about what really happened the day Tyler's truck almost crushed her; she has given up a happy life in warm Phoenix and come to live in cold, rainy Forks, a place she clearly hates; and she gets close enough to notice things about Edward—his changing eye color, for instance. But because he can't hear what she's thinking, he'll have to talk to her to better understand her.

At first Bella thinks Edward is simply a mysteriously beautiful teenager, but it doesn't take long for her to wonder if there isn't more to his story. Edward doesn't act like other humans, after all. He appears to hate her for no reason at all; he comes out of nowhere to save her life; his eyes change color daily; he has an old-fashioned way of speaking; and he's just *too* beautiful, too graceful. But to solve this puzzle, Bella will have to talk to Edward.

Anyone who believes communication makes love less compelling hasn't listened in on Bella and Edward's lunch-time talks, heard their discussion over dinner in Port Angeles, or spied on them in the meadow. During these conversations, Bella and Edward finally begin to see each other as they really are, and they like what they see: Edward the vampire who doesn't want to be a monster ("he's even more unbelievable *behind* the face") and Bella the vulnerable but brave human with almost no instinct for self-preservation. Finally, Bella can understand Edward's struggle and make sense out of his mood swings—he *doesn't* have a multiple personality disorder. Edward begins to see that Bella is tougher than she looks— she isn't going to run away from him screaming.

Their new knowledge of each other doesn't shut the door to love; on the contrary, it allows it to develop. On the one hand, these conversations help them to learn *how* to love one another: just how much skin contact Bella's heart and

Edward's self-control can take. One the other hand, these early conversations help them begin to look past the categories "vampire" and "human" (read "dominant" and "subordinate"). Once Bella realizes that Edward is a vampire and she decides that this fact doesn't matter to her, and once Edward accepts that Bella is just as attached to him as he is to her, then for a short time they are able simply to enjoy their luck in finding each other: holding hands, making out, joking around.

Risk and Transformation

But things soon change as their relationship puts them at risk. When James's coven recognizes that Bella is human and Edward moves to defend her, the game (literally) is up. Suddenly, the differences between Bella the human and Edward the vampire take center stage, and these differences are quickly construed as inequalities. Bella is weak, frail, and vulnerable; Edward is strong, fast, and lethal. As these inequalities are emphasized, their once frequent and intimate conversations notably diminish—Edward decides to leave Forks without even discussing it with Bella. Because communication makes it difficult to participate in a relationship built on dominance and subordination, perhaps it's not surprising that Bella and Edward stop talking. In fact, it isn't until Bella saves Edward from the Volturi and evens things up that we start to see the kinds of conversations that we did earlier.

It's in these post-Italy conversations about sex and marriage, souls and vampires, safety and werewolves, Victoria and the Volturi that Bella and Edward recognize that they differ beyond just their chromosomal count. But it's in these conversations that we also see their love endure and deepen. As they explore their different needs and desires, they show us how communication even in the face of disagreement and pain can bring people closer together. Edward and Bella become closer in part as they learn to treat each other as equals: It's as a result of these conversations that Edward comes to see that his attitude toward Bella and the were-wolves is misplaced; that they learn to negotiate compromises; and that they untangle the questions of sex, marriage, and vampire existence.

Bella and Edward do not emerge from *Breaking Dawn* as they began in *Twilight*. But it is less the venom that transforms Bella into a vampire than their increasing honesty and communication that marks the difference. God knows, Bella and Edward do not have a perfectly equal relationship—Edward can still be controlling and Bella really needs to see herself more clearly—but it's these imperfections that make this unbelievable story believable—and it's the sustained attempts to resolve these imperfections that give us hope for our own relationships.

NOTES

1. bell hooks, *All About Love: New Visions* (New York: HarperCollins Press, 2001), p. 97.

2. Donna Chung, "Violence, Control, Romance and Gender Inequality: Young Women and Heterosexual Relationships," in *Women's Studies International Forum* 28: 449, 2005.

3. See Andrea Dworkin, *Intercourse: 20th Anniversary Edition* (New York: Basic Books, 2006).

4. Stephenie Meyer, *Eclipse* (New York: Little, Brown and Company, 2007), pp. 223–224.

5. Stephenie Meyer, *Twilight* (New York: Little, Brown and Company, 2005), p. 328.

6. Stephenie Meyer, *New Moon* (New York: Little, Brown and Company, 2006), pp. 512–513.

7. *Eclipse*, pp. 148–149.

8. Following her lead, we will not capitalize "bell hooks." She's right about so much, she's probably right about capitalization, too.

9. *Eclipse*, p. 143.

10. *Eclipse*, p. 190.

11. *Eclipse*, p. 617.

12. hooks, *All About Love*, p. 157.

13. Ibid.

THE "REAL" DANGER: FACT VS. FICTION FOR THE GIRL AUDIENCE

Rebecca Housel

The newspaper headline screams: "Eighteen-Year-Old Slain by Husband after Giving Birth." As you continue reading, you learn that the young woman was brainwashed by a strange blood-drinking cult who call themselves a "family," though none of the members were actually related. The young woman's husband was much older than she and had a history of violence. In fact, you learn that her husband used to stalk her prior to their marriage, watching her secretly from the woods near her home and climbing into an unsecured window at night to watch her sleep without her knowledge. Once the young woman, then seventeen, was initiated into a relationship with the man and his "family," she was encouraged to marry right after her high school graduation. The young woman reportedly had bruises all over her body after returning from their honeymoon, where she also reportedly became pregnant. Her husband was not happy about the pregnancy and wanted her to have an abortion. She refused, eventually leading to him ripping the child from her womb, then, draining her of her blood until she finally stopped breathing.

Sounds torturous and sick, doesn't it? But in fact, this is the basis of a tween-teen literary phenomenon called the *Twilight* saga. Painted with the romantic, *fictitious* flourish of author Stephenie Meyer's pen, what in reality would be a horrific account of violence against women, all too familiar in today's media, becomes a dangerously romanticized fantasy for a primarily young female audience.

And what exactly is confronting the female audience of Meyer's *Twilight*? Current statistics on violence against women in the United States and elsewhere tell a truly horrifying story—they also suggest that putting forward this kind of fiction is dangerous, perhaps even irresponsible. Using Jean Baudrillard's (1929–2007) theories on the effects of simulating reality, as well as contemporary psychologist Jean M. Twenge's findings on what she calls "Generation Me" (anyone born in the early 1970s through the 1990s), we will better understand how and where the popular culture of *Twilight* intersects with philosophy. Maybe, just maybe, reason will render the latest vampire craze in pop culture toothless, saving millions of young girls from victimization while they impossibly seek their own Edwards.

Just the Facts, Ma'am

Who will the female audience really find when looking for Edward, after separating the fact from the fiction? I guarantee, it will not be a handsome, rich vampire looking for a soul mate. In fact, he will be a possessive, dangerously violent stalker—the same man who perpetuates statistics like these every year in the United States:

- 85 percent of women who are stalked know their stalker; 76 percent of women killed by intimate partners were also stalked by their intimate partners.[1]
- According to the U.S. Department of Justice, Office on Violence Against Women, the most recent Stalking Victimization Report shows that in a twelve-month period an estimated 3.4 million women age eighteen or older are victims of stalking; only 60 percent report victimization to police.[2]

There are even more hard-to-believe statistics regarding the pandemic known as violence against women (VAW). The World Health Organization (WHO) completed a ten-country study and found that 71 percent of women reported physical or sexual violence by a husband or intimate partner, noting that violence against women is a "major public health problem and violation of human rights," and that "violence by an intimate partner is one of the most common forms of violence against women."[3]

But what does "stalking" mean? What exactly is "violence against women"? The U.S. Department of Justice defines two or more of the following behaviors as stalking:

- Unwanted calls, letters, or e-mails to the victim
- Showing up at a place where the stalker had no reason to be in order to see, follow, spy on, or otherwise engage the victim
- Waiting for the victim at home, school, work, the grocery store, or other frequented areas
- Leaving unwanted items for the victim
- Following or spying on the victim

Edward Cullen is guilty of at least three of the above criteria; it doesn't matter that Bella Swan may like such attentions—that only speaks to Bella's naiveté and lack of experience. Any man who climbs through your window at night to watch you sleep is a stalker by any definition. Note that the definitions use the word "victim." This is because in real life Bella would be considered a *victim* of stalking, a criminal behavior that often escalates to violence against the victim, even death—and the audience sees this with Bella and Edward, but through the rose-colored glasses provided by Stephenie Meyer's romanticized version.

In 2005, the year *Twilight* was first published, 1,181 women were murdered in the United States by an intimate partner—an average of three women per day. Young women like Bella are disproportionately the victims of domestic violence. More than ten years after the Violence Against Women Act (VAWA) of 1994, statistics for 2005 still show that one-third of all women murdered (three each day!), are killed by intimate partners. That's simply outrageous. When you factor in how Meyer's books have influenced millions of female tweens and teens, we may theorize if not an increase, certainly not a lessening of such VAW statistics as the girl audience grows up and pursues the "man of their dreams," shaped in part by the fantasized image of Edward. Still not convinced? There's more.

The U.S. Department of Justice offers the definition of violence against women, also referred to as "domestic violence," as including physical abuse, sexual abuse, emotional abuse, economic abuse, and/or psychological abuse. We know Bella has bruises all over her body after her first sexual encounter with Edward. We also know that because of her relationship with Edward, Bella's life is constantly threatened, resulting in other cuts, bruises, even broken bones.

The stress of being in that situation can cause even fictional characters psychological injury. The Department of Justice defines psychological abuse as fear and intimidation by threatening physical harm to self or partner, children, or partner's friends and family, as well as forcing isolation from family, friends, work, and/or school. If we were to be honest readers not taken in by the romance, isn't that what happens to Bella? Doesn't she begin to feel isolated from her family and friends? In fact, her relationship with Edward requires Bella to die in order to live with Edward. In other words, Bella has to completely change who she is, where she lives, and who her friends are. She changes her plans for college and isolates herself from her family.

The emotional abuse Bella suffers is the undermining of her self-worth as a mortal human being; she wants, even begs for, death. Yes, in Bella's imagination death is to be transformative, binding her to Edward forever. But in reality, death is not like that. It's irreparable, permanent. Many women experiencing domestic violence by an intimate partner do not report the violence or abuse because, like victims of kidnapping with Stockholm Syndrome, the abused begin to relate to their abusers. Because the relationship is already an intimate or a "love" relationship, women are also vulnerable to what the Department of Justice calls economic abuse. Bella is a victim of this as well.

Economic abuse occurs when an abuser makes or attempts to make a victim financially dependent by maintaining economic control. Bella is not from a wealthy family; Edward is. Edward buys Bella new cars and designer clothes, takes her on expensive trips without even a second thought, and offers to pay for her education at an Ivy League school, among other things. While seemingly generous, because it is all couched in the understanding on the part of an almost one-hundred-year-old man that Bella has to die, the "generosity" becomes part of the attempt to isolate Bella, making her feel completely dependent on Edward.

Even Edward's attempt to commit suicide fits the definition of emotional abuse and is part of the overall violence against Bella, a young mortal girl from a lower-income, divorced home with little adult supervision—the perfect victim. But Bella is also a victim of her generation.

Bella and "Generation Me"

In her book *Generation Me*, Jean M. Twenge discusses a series of psychological studies showing a shift in the social "ethos" (a universally accepted culture or philosophy) of people born in the 1970s through the 1990s, referred to as "Generation Me" or "GenMe."[4] As Twenge sees it, GenMe is unapologetically about the self. Stephenie Meyer, born in 1973, is at the beginning of GenMe; but she was no less influenced by, and now is a part of, the concerted social effort to focus more on how special an individual is through everything from elementary school curricula to the pop culture all around us, including Meyer's *Twilight* books and the resulting film franchise. So what's wrong with feeling like you're special and focusing on yourself?

Well, once GenMe hits adulthood, or begins to recognize adulthood in their tween-teen years, misery is the result. Twenge's research suggests that GenMe has the highest number of individuals on antidepressants at younger ages and also has the highest suicide rates.[5] GenMe also has an increased tendency toward narcissism, an intriguing and pertinent connection to *Twilight*'s Bella.

Narcissism, a term originally coined by Sigmund Freud (1856–1939), describes a psychological dysfunction or personality disorder of excessive self-love. The condition is named after the myth of Narcissus, who gazed at his reflection in a pool of water with such concentration and interest that he could do nothing else. Needless to say, he died.[6] While Freud felt that a certain amount of self-love was healthy, narcissism begets a lack of empathy for others, an exaggerated sense of entitlement, and an excessive selfishness. Only the self matters, nothing else. Bella exhibits classic narcissism in her choices throughout the *Twilight* saga, showing that her character not only is a reflection of GenMe, but also expresses the crux of the GenMe problem: Concerned only with the self and the self's desires, GenMe becomes seriously disillusioned when reality corrects their inflated self-image. GenMe feels no need for approval, taking for granted their "specialness." Unfortunately, the rest of the world does not always agree with GenMe's perceptions, resulting in deep disappointment, depression, and ironically, self-doubt.

Twenge argues that the baby boomer generation (those born from 1945–1963), who were themselves once referred to as the "me generation," have a very different take on the self. The self-image for boomers was not handed to them by parents, teachers, or relatives, but was earned through hard work: "I'm good at writing because I worked at it and then got published in a national magazine" versus the GenMe's take: "I'm good at writing because I'm special and it does not matter what other people think; I don't have to achieve publishing success to know I'm good."

Divorce is part of the shift in our social ethos toward individuality and away from abstract duty: "My marriage commitment is not as important as my happiness." For the children of divorce, compensation is both a sweet reward and an ultimate punishment. Parents attempting to "normalize" life for a child of divorce often will do the opposite—equally spoiling that child in attempts to make the child feel special despite the state of that child's family—creating a unique contradiction. While Bella's mother, Renee, certainly loves Bella, she makes choices that exclude Bella. In order for Bella to continue to feel special as an individual, she must move to a different part of the country, away from her home, school, and friends. In order for Bella to continue to feel special despite being rejected by one parent and forced to leave everything she knows that supports her feelings of specialness, Bella must create a new social network among total strangers (not an easy feat), or find a way to separate herself from the crowd—and she does just that through her relationship with Edward.

So how is Bella narcissistic when she seems to consistently focus on how average she is, how clumsy, how uninteresting? (Though it's clear to the reader that Bella is exactly the opposite, given the attentions of multiple boys from her new school—both living and dead.) She may be focusing on how average she seems to be, but the point is that she is *always* focusing on herself. Her choice to be with Edward is to feed her curiosity, at any expense. She realizes early on that Edward is dangerous, but continues to gravitate toward him because she *wants* to. Even after the almost fatal episode with James, Bella continues to choose what psychologists might term a "toxic relationship" with Edward because it is something she *desires*. Her father does not approve of Edward. Even her flaky mother is concerned. Bella's new friends are also cautious. But Bella continues anyway. She begins to seek Edward out. When she learns that Edward has been watching her sleep at night and following her around in secret, she is flattered—Edward's actions feed in to Bella's GenMe narcissistic tendencies and focus. And that kind of vulnerability is the problem with narcissism.

The excess of self-love and self-indulgence can lead to dangerous, even fatal, choices in pursuit of *doing what one wants simply because one wants to.* There is no thought of duty to family, of how others may feel, of how certain decisions will irreparably alter the lives of people Bella supposedly loves. Bella's singular thought is how to get whom she wants (Edward) and how to get what she wants (to stay with Edward forever). In her pursuit of immortality, a privilege Bella feels entitled to simply because she wants it, Bella justifies her desires through her belief that her death will only increase her specialness.[7] Classic GenMe: "I'm about to die, but that's okay because I'll be even more special than I already am and that's all that matters." Of course, one's specialness is *not* all that matters, and that is where reality hits GenMe hard in the face.

Enter Jean Baudrillard's ideas on the dangers of simulating reality.

Twilight in the Desert of the Real

A simulacrum is a false image or artificial representation translated from reality to a medium such as literature, film, television, art, music, radio, or other. Much of our popular culture is nothing more than a collection of these representations of reality or simulacra. The simulation of reality leads to simulacra, and simulacra blur the lines between what is real and what we believe to be real.[8] Yes, GenMe is still in full force here, as well. In fact, both Twenge's GenMe and Baudrillard's simulacrum come from a universal shift in social thought from modernism to postmodernism. The basics are that modernism stemmed from a social consensus that there was one truth, while postmodernism is based on the belief that every perspective is not only valuable but valid—multiple truths are now accepted and acceptable. Consider this in light of Twenge's ideas on baby boomers versus GenMe. Boomers, born on the heels of World War II, were part of a social "ethos" believing in duty to the whole, a focus on community, while GenMe is focused on the self or the validity and value of their own unique perspectives.[9]

Meyer's *Twilight* saga is part of the simulacra perpetuated through popular culture. The characters simulate teenagers, typical parents, neighbors, friends, and relatives. With settings that are real, such as Arizona, Washington, or Italy, the audience buys in to the simulation of real life further. Even the relationships between the characters seem conceptually believable, or real. But the simulation isn't of anything real—and that's the catch. There are no vampires. There are no werewolves. There are no good stalkers and murderers. A simulacrum is a copy without an original. Baudrillard cautions that simulation welcomes a "liquidation" of reality—and he's not alone.[10]

Loren Coleman's book *The Copycat Effect: How the Media and Popular Culture Trigger the Mayhem in Tomorrow's Headlines* (2004) discusses a number of social phenomena including cults, teen suicides, and school shootings that follow the idea: "If it bleeds, it leads," pointing to what Coleman refers to as a "Death Orientation" in media.[11] *Twilight* fits the "if it bleeds, it leads" death-orientation profile. Of course, *Twilight* is softened by teen romance and the allure of the vampire. But it's the simulation of the story, particularly powerful on the silver screen, which makes the younger audience buy in to the idea that there really are "good" abusive relationships. A simulacrum of love emerges, and reality disappears. The reality of a relationship with a "real" man like Edward, as seen through the staggering VAW statistics, is far from the "truth" represented in *Twilight*. There's no romance in stalking. There's no love in bruises. There's nothing remotely romantic or loving about being killed.

I love a good story as much as the next person; my caveat here is not about writing books like *Twilight* or the creation of movies with similar themes, but to the female audience being taken in by the ideas of reality represented in the books and the films. Recognizing the power of books and film is not new; both have been used to perpetuate social ideas, even propaganda. Early filmmakers who started Hollywood studios such as Paramount and MGM deliberately inserted ideas about acceptance and assimilation for the mass audience in hopes of mass acceptance.[12] Books such as Chuck Klosterman's *Sex, Drugs, and Cocoa Puffs* (2004) illustrate how movie stars like John Cusack became simulacra, representations of what a "real" boyfriend was supposed to be for GenX and early GenMe women.[13] Twenge's book on GenMe discusses in detail how influential the media and popular culture can be on audiences as young as eighteen months old. It's important not to take for granted that members of the younger *Twilight* girl audience are truly buying in to the simulation as not just a simulation, but as something attainable, something real. But hope springs eternal in the movies; there's hope for the girl audience yet!

New Moon Rising?

The questions that surround the *Twilight* phenomenon often focus on whether or not Bella is a feminist hero: Is she being assertive and going after what she wants, or is she submissive to the greater power of an older man, a predator by all counts? Why Bella should choose Jacob Black, or why Edward is the better choice. Such questions, though, are irrelevant without first understanding what is behind the *Twilight* concept.

Before we can look at Bella as an individual, we must study where she comes from, how the whole of society helped to shape the individual—and since Bella is a fictional character created by the real Stephenie Meyer, it makes sense to follow the social attitudes that shaped Meyer's own individuality. Malcolm Gladwell calls this idea the "Power of Context" in his book *The Tipping Point* (2000). Showing how small ideas become social phenomena with a definite "tipping point," where the idea catches on with larger society, Gladwell discusses how understanding the context or history of an idea, a person, or a situation is very powerful in terms of understanding social trends.[14] In every way possible, Meyer's *Twilight* concept and following books, films, and related merchandise had a tipping point that led to incredible popularity.

Meyer created the quintessential female fantasy in Edward, a "boy" who is really older and much more mature than he looks; who loves Bella for who she is and not what she looks like; who wants to sleep with Bella but not in a sexual way; who is protective and very, very rich, with a loving, supportive family who totally accept Bella, regardless of the clear educational and economic differences. Really, what's not to like? It's the reason girls and women from eight to forty-eight are crazy about Edward. But there is an innate danger to buying in to the romanticized version of the "ideal" man as described by Meyer. Edward's character fits the description of what in real life would pose a real mortal danger to women: possessive stalkers who perpetrate rampant violence against women worldwide.

In any world other than the fantastical one created by Meyer, Edward would be jailed. Bella's police chief father would have issued a restraining order against Edward. Edward even follows the psychology of abusers, with periods of blissful happiness followed by periods of severe abuse: He has to be cruel to Bella so that she understands what he needs her to understand; he has to make a suicide attempt when he believes Bella has moved on; he can't help the bruises he inflicts on Bella during their first sexual encounter; he has to kill Bella after she has the baby in order to save her. In the context of Meyer's world, Edward's otherwise illegal and immoral actions are justified, but the female audience exposed to this fantasy needs to understand that in reality, Edward is not the ideal boyfriend-lover. In fact, Jacob is.

Jacob encourages Bella to be herself, regardless of how it affects him, regardless of what he wants. He never threatens her. He supports her no matter what, even when it is in direct conflict with his own desires. He respects Bella as a person and truly wants to make her happy, even if it means watching her become the pet of a vampire and his family. He's the only one who stands up to Bella when she endangers her life in pursuit of Edward, risking the friendship Jacob values more than anything else, because Jacob is *truly* Bella's friend.[15]

Girls, *that* is the kind of person you need to find! Looking for Edward will only lead to black eyes, rape, torture, and possibly even death. Take it from a real-life Bella who found a "real" Edward—you don't want that. You want respect, support, friendship—all of which adds up to true love. Luckily, my Edward didn't succeed in his attempt to kill me, and I was able to find my Jacob. Don't be fooled by the fancy bells and whistles offered by the simulacra in *Twilight*. Don't let a bunch of publicists and marketing directors searching for a tipping point influence your definition of reality. Understand the power of the context behind *Twilight* and its author. As a card-carrying member of GenMe, I understand it is all too easy to be fooled into satisfying our own desires for how we want life to be. Being lucky enough to have lived beyond eighteen and proudly maintaining my mortality, there is no hesitation when I say emphatically that living a long life is good; living a long life with a Jacob is great. Want something even better?

Earning the specialness you take for granted is more fulfilling than you can imagine. Fantasy only provides the facade of specialness. Go for the "real" sparkle; you don't need to have skin like diamonds to do it. You don't need designer clothes or a fancy car. You just need a challenge to conquer.

And now you have one.

NOTES

1. From the National Center for Victims of Crime statistics, www.ncvc.org.

2. See www.ovw.usdoj.gov.

3. See www.who.int/mediacentre/factsheets/fs239/en/.

4. Jean M. Twenge, *Generation Me: Why Today's Young Americans Are More Confident, Assertive, Entitled—and More Miserable than Ever Before* (New York: Free Press, 2006). Note that another label, used for people born after 1963 and through the early 1970s, is "Gen X." Gen X-ers are known for being classic slackers who still have a knack for achievement; for example, Gen X is often associated with the dot.com boom. Essentially, early GenMe populations born in the late 1960s and early 1970s are on the blurry borderline of Gen X and GenMe. From personal experience, I would say that we seem to have gotten the best of both worlds.

5. Ibid., p. 104.

6. Narcissus was then turned into the flower of the same name; it should be noted, however, that there are multiple versions of the tale of Narcissus with variations on the same theme of self-love and resulting death.

7. Meyer makes a point of having Bella question her destiny throughout the *Twilight* saga; Bella often feels she is destined to die young and repeatedly uses this logical fallacy

to persuade Edward to kill her. Her belief that she is destined to die young is just that—a belief. It is not based on anything real outside of Bella's knack of being in the wrong place at the wrong time—much of which is because of her relationship with Edward.

8. Jean Baudrillard, *Simulacra and Simulation*, trans. Sheila Faria Glaser (Ann Arbor: University of Michigan Press, 1994), pp. 80–81.

9. It should be noted that the parents of GenMe are typically baby boomers; however, children born in the late 1980s could conceivably be children of early GenMe individuals. It was the boomers, though, who initially created the social supports Twenge lists in her book as the major reason for the self-focus in GenMe. Along those lines, the reader should be aware that studies are based on only a percentage of any population and do not accurately represent every individual associated with a particular generation.

10. Baudrillard, *Simulacra and Simulation*, p. 2.

11. Loren Coleman, *The Copycat Effect: How the Media and Popular Culture Trigger the Mayhem in Tomorrow's Headlines* (New York: Pocket Books, 2004), pp. 7–11.

12. See Neal Gabler's *An Empire of Their Own: How the Jews Invented Hollywood* (New York: Anchor Books, 1989).

13. See Chuck Klosterman's memoir, *Sex, Drugs, and Cocoa Puffs* (New York: Scribner, 2004) for more.

14. Malcolm Gladwell, *The Tipping Point: How Little Things Can Make a Big Difference* (Boston: Little, Brown and Company, 2000).

15. Because the yin and yang flow into each other, even when Jacob argues or gets angry, it's just a natural extension of that flow; in other words, every yin has a bit of yang and every yang has a bit of yin. The two are inseparable in their co-existence. There can never be one without the other. See chapter 18, "The Tao of Jacob," for more.

PART FOUR

BREAKING DAWN

fourteen

TWILIGHT OF AN IDOL: OUR FATAL ATTRACTION TO VAMPIRES

Jennifer L. McMahon

Twilight, like some of the best examples of vampire fiction, both celebrates and critiques the creature upon which it focuses. It's easy to see what's wrong with bloodsuckers, but what makes them so appealing? The answer is simple: wish fulfillment. Human desire is the basis for the vampire mystique. While vampires remain horrific by virtue of their transgressive acts, we nonetheless desire to be like them. But why is that? As we'll see, existential philosophy offers an explanation for our fascination with vampires and suggests that it is a love we may want to bury.

An Undying Wish

The existential philosopher Martin Heidegger (1889–1976) argued that humans fear death more than anything else.

Although other things can inspire fear, nothing arouses it like our mortality. Indeed, Heidegger suggested that most commonplace fears derive from, and are psychological substitutes for, our fear of death.[1] According to Heidegger, humans display a unique concern for being that stems primarily from the fact that we know we are finite. This awareness is the foundation for existential "angst."[2] Throughout our lives, humans seek "flight from death," or at least "tranquillization about death," and the anxiety that we have about our mortality inspires a desire for immortality.[3] Here lies the appeal of the vampire. Vampires are immortal. They personify our desire to elude death. Blood is a potent symbol of life, and beings who ingest blood are figures who control life and symbolize the immortal gods that Jean-Paul Sartre (1905–1980) argued we all desire to be.[4]

Twilight clearly illustrates our anxiety over mortality. At the end of *Twilight*, after Edward Cullen saves Bella Swan, she laments that he did not let James's venom transform her into a vampire. Although she is happy to have escaped a violent death, she despairs because Edward's rescue is temporary. In rescuing her, he damns her to eventual death. Bella cries, "I'm going to die . . . every minute of the day I get closer."[5] Although Edward and Jacob Black try to convince Bella that death is natural, she states, "I was . . . eager to trade mortality for immortality."[6] She asks, "What [is] so great about mortality?" and regrets that Edward is wedded to an idea "as stupid as leaving [her] human."[7] She describes transformation into a vampire positively—even religiously—as a "conversion that [will] set [her] free from [her] mortality."[8]

Although our own mortality tends to be of greatest concern, we suffer the mortality of others, too. Both because we would be injured by their death and we want those we love "to live a long, full life," we desire their immortality.[9] This desire to extend immortality to others is also illustrated in *Twilight*. Carlisle Cullen creates the members of his family not only for companionship, but also to save them from the "horrible . . . waste" of premature death.[10] He works as a physician not just as "penance," but also to forestall human fatality.[11] Likewise, Bella's agony over Renesmee's "racing age" is expressive of her fear that her child will be stolen from her by death.[12] Bella expresses indescribable "happiness" at the discovery that Renesmee will not die and that she, Edward, and Renesmee "ha[ve] forever . . . together."[13]And of course, Edward and Bella seek to love each other not until "death do they part," but for forever. Clearly, vampires personify our desire to spare not only ourselves, but also our loved ones the horror of death.

Deadly Transformations

The appeal of vampires is not simply a function of their immortality. They compensate for other anxieties. One is aging. Although aging is fearful as a harbinger of death, it arouses anxiety in its own right. Sartre examined the anxiety that individuals have about their embodiment, anxiety rooted in the fact that humans are both consciousness and body. While he was clear that "the body is a necessary characteristic" of consciousness, he argued that consciousness feels "separated from it."[14] In fact, consciousness lacks coincidence with anything. While this lack makes awareness and freedom possible, it also makes consciousness feel estranged from its body. This body is subject not merely to change, but also to decay. The proverbial ghost in the machine, the mind can do nothing but bear anxious witness to the progressive aging of the body and the concomitant deterioration of its own function. This compels the feeling not only of "nausea," but also of terror.[15]

Aging arouses anxiety not only because it is outside conscious control and yields diminished performance, but also because we idealize youth. We decry aging because it moves us away from our ideal state toward an undesirable end. As Albert Camus (1913–1960), stated wonderfully, "[A] day comes when a man notices [that] . . . [h]e belongs to time, and by the horror that seizes him, he recognizes his worst enemy."[16] The march of time is particularly distasteful, because today "youth is no longer viewed as a transitory state . . . but [as] an aspiration, a vaunted condition in which, if one [could] arrange it, [one would] settle in perpetuity."[17]

Twilight expresses our concern about aging and our wish to escape it. Because Bella seeks a long-term relationship with an immortal vampire, she expresses more concern over aging than most teens. She states that "age is a touchy subject," and when she discovers that Edward, his family, and Jacob are exempt from aging, she screams furiously, "'Not . . . aging? Is that a joke?' . . . Tears—tears of rage—filled my eyes. . . . 'Am I the only one who has to get old? I get older every stinking day! . . . Damn it! What kind of world is this? Where's the justice?'"[18]

Bella's anxiety over aging is expressed again in a dream in *New Moon*. The dream opens with Bella imagining her Grandma Marie meeting Edward. The dream transforms into a "nightmare" when Bella realizes that she is the "ancient, creased, and withered" woman who stands next to the eternally youthful vampire.[19] She wakes from the dream in terror, describing time as a thief "lurk[ing] in ambush."[20] She cries, "I could feel it—I was older. Every day I got older . . . [and] worse."[21] For Bella, aging is synonymous with "wast[ing]."[22] This leads Bella to express "horror"[23] at the prospect of turning thirty, and to tell Edward that being frozen forever at the age of eighteen is "every woman's dream."[24] At the end of the saga, Bella is transformed into a vampire and absolved of the indignity of aging. Clearly, the appeal of vampires lies not only in their immortality, but also in their eternal youth.

Unbreakable

Mortality and aging are not the only problems that people have with embodiment. Bodies have other "weaknesse[s]" that we seek to overcome.[25] Although our bodies are possessed of many wonderful abilities, they are also vulnerable. We suffer extremes of cold and heat. We are easily injured. Minor falls can break bones. Simple accidents can cause injuries that demand emergency care. Our susceptibility to injury compels a desire for the superhuman bodies that vampires possess.

Twilight expresses the anxiety we have about our bodies. These anxieties make it easy to sympathize with Bella, the charming, yet comically clumsy teen.[26] As Edward and Jacob Black repeatedly remind Bella, she is "incredibly breakable."[27] Bella couldn't agree more. She repeatedly declares that it is "too dangerous to be human."[28] *Twilight* contrasts human susceptibility to injury with the invulnerability of vampires in numerous scenes. Bella's injury at the hands of James,[29] her nearly fatal finger slice on her birthday,[30] and the unintentional injuries she receives from Edward on their honeymoon express the vulnerability of humans as clearly as the general notion of humans as "prey."[31]

By personifying "virtual indestructibility,"[32] the vampires in the *Twilight* saga illustrate our deep-seated desire for less susceptible bodies. Where humans are composed of "brittle,"[33] "warm, breakable"[34] flesh, vampire skin is "hard,"[35] cold, and likened to "stone"[36] and "steel."[37] Rather than be subject to damage, vampires impart it. Contact with a vampire easily bruises human skin, breaks bone, and even dents metal. Though not immune to destruction, there are "very few ways that [vampires] can be killed."[38] Indeed, they, and the werewolves, are nearly indestructible.

Bloody Special

Vampires are appealing not simply because of their indestructibility, but also because of their special powers. Like the superheroes from Marvel Comics, the vampires in *Twilight* are possessed of superhuman strength and speed. They can swim the ocean and run hundreds of miles with ease. They leap canyons with catlike grace and crush rock effortlessly into powder. Personifying our desire, Bella seeks to trade her "human and weak" body for one with "superpower[s]."[39] She thirsts for the expanded senses, "infallible . . . mind," and unique "gift[s]" of the vampires.[40] One such special gift is beauty. Perhaps nothing is emphasized more consistently in the *Twilight* saga than Edward's physical appeal. He is described again and again as "devastatingly" beautiful. And Edward is not unique. Beauty is a standard characteristic of vampires. We find vampires appealing because they embody the ideal of beauty to which we aspire and which exerts considerable influence. Bella wants to become a vampire partly because she knows her transformation will render her "inhumanly beautiful." We love vampires because they exemplify a standard of beauty to which we aspire, "an ideal so remote from our daily affairs that its exemplars seem to belong to another species."[41]

Vampires feed our thirst to be special in another way. Sartre and his fellow existentialists agreed that a major cause of human anxiety is our lack of necessity. We see concern over meaning in *Twilight* when Bella denies that she possesses any special abilities and scoffs at the notion that she could be the object of undying love. Regardless, she captures Edward's heart, commanding his affection so powerfully that, like Romeo, he declares that he will not live without her. In addition, she ends up being a central figure in an epic battle and the unsuspecting savior of the vampires from the Volturi. Bella expresses our own latent wish to escape anonymity and ascend to a state of supreme significance.

Lone Wolves

Though not as obvious as our desire to avoid injury or obscurity, another weakness individuals seek to avoid is their vulnerability to others. As both Heidegger and Sartre asserted, humans are fundamentally social. Though Heidegger argued that we normally take comfort in others, Sartre was alert to the potential that our relationships have to arouse anxiety. Interpersonal relations cause anxiety because of the danger that others represent and the unique dependence that individuals have on one another.[42] Other people can injure us physically and psychologically. They can take what we want or interfere with our plans. We don't know who represents a threat because we do not know what others are thinking.

Philosophers call this the problem of other minds. While people can tell us what they are thinking, they don't always do this. We don't like this! Vampires, though, can read minds. The vampires in the *Twilight* saga derive additional appeal from this ability. Although they are subject to some limitations, they are all able to see into the minds of others, with one exception: Bella. Bella's mind operates like a shield. In combination, Bella and the vampires articulate an understandable wish with respect to others. More often than not, we would like to be able to know what others are thinking; however, we do not want them to be able to do the same.

Of course, it is not only the minds of others that compel concern. Others are also anxiety-provoking because of the dependence that we have upon them. Existentialists pay special attention to this reliance and the concern that it arouses. Rather than being only temporary, our dependence on others is permanent. Sartre argued that one of the things we depend on others for is our own identity. Challenging the traditional notion of essential self, he explained how our engagement with others prompts self-reflection, a prerequisite for personal identity, and how personal identity is established initially through the internalization, and later through the critical appropriation, of the objective characterizations that others provide.

Our dependence on others would not be so troubling were it not for the nature of consciousness; namely, the fact that it never feels identical with anything. The ability to dissociate from what we perceive is the foundation of human subjectivity and agency; however, when someone characterizes us as clumsy or talented, fit or fat, they are characterizing us as something fixed, not free. Of course, people cannot help that. They engage with us as the bodies that we are. Nonetheless, because consciousness tends to resist any objective characterization it hasn't chosen, the fact that others judge us as "ordinary object[s]" is a source of irritation and anxiety.[43]

Twilight expresses this anxiety clearly. Bella's adolescent social anxiety, her perennial concern that others will see her as strange or unattractive, is an exaggerated representation of the concern for others that most people experience throughout their lives. Whether agonizing over being the new outsider in Forks, or tripping in gym class, Bella recognizes that her self-esteem hinges on the recognition and validation of others and feels fragile because of this dependence.

A significant part of the fascination we have with vampires comes from the fact that their relationships differ radically from ours. Most vampires are loners; they do not need others the way we do. But vampires do need humans—they need them for food. As Bella remarks after her transformation, her urgent need for Jacob "had vanished . . . a human weakness."[44] Vampires personify the desire to ascend to "another plane of being" where we are no longer affected by "constant concern" for other people.[45] Others are reduced to means, indeed, to *meals*. Vampires do not have to curb their impulses to gain social acceptance. Instead, they embody our desire for "absolute freedom," our wish to be "master of the situation," "to get hold of [another person] and reduce [him] to being subject . . . to my freedom."[46]

Tortuous Thirsts

The biting of humans and drinking of blood are alluring for even less savory reasons than social control. Although the violent seizure of human blood is the basis for the horror we associate with vampires, it is also elemental to their appeal. In violating social taboos against murder and cannibalism, vampires personify our desire for an absolute surrender to instinct. Although this wish seems inconsistent with the desire for control, Sartre argued that these divergent wants are anchored in the unhappy nature of human consciousness. As he explained, the possession of reflexive consciousness puts humans in a unique position with respect to their instincts. While we are nothing other than highly evolved animals affected by natural impulses, our consciousness gives us the ability to decide whether we are going to act on those impulses or not. While this makes us free, it places a burden on us.

Because humans often experience freedom as anguish, we often seek to escape our nature by trying to be a pure subject or a pure object, a free agent or a determined thing. Sartre called these efforts "bad faith." Our desire for absolute control is expressive of the desire to ascend to the level of pure subject. Our desire to surrender to instinct is expressive of our wish to escape our freedom.

Vampires are compelling because they personify command and surrender simultaneously. They represent both "dependence and rapaciousness."[47] They are at once masters of others *and* subjects to their own thirst. In their absolute abandon to appetite, vampires express our latent wish to surrender to instinct. They embody our desire to indulge our aggressive impulses, sate hunger and thirst, and of course, "lose [ourselves]" in pleasures like sex without the awful sting of conscience.[48]

All guilty pleasures to be sure, but not everything about *Twilight* is.

The Not-So-Guilty Pleasures of *Twilight*

The vampires in *Twilight* do deviate from the archetypal vampire in important ways. They are undeterred by garlic and invulnerable to stakes through the heart. They don't sleep in coffins—indeed, they don't sleep at all. Daylight isn't deadly, either. Instead, vampires glisten in it. Most important, they aren't exactly monstrous. The Cullens and the Denali clan are kinder, gentler vampires. What distinguishes them most from the stereotypical bloodsucker is the fact that they curb their natural thirst for human blood. This makes the vampires in *Twilight* especially compelling because it exempts them from being murderers (which lets us feel less guilty about our attraction to them), and because it allows them to personify the ambivalence that we have about our appetites.

As philosophers from the time of Plato have argued, the appetites have the potential to compromise the function of reason. Sartre argued that our appetites and desires are essential aspects of our being, even though consciousness does not normally identify with them. Instead, it tends to see them as alien forces that threaten its autonomy from the inside. We fear losing our selves and our humanity to our bodily impulses.

Vampires are captivating because they simultaneously depict our desire to dominate impulse and our desire to surrender to it. Clearly, vampires articulate the anxiety that we have about appetites. Vampires are beings who are defined by thirst. This thirst robs them of their humanity. They are made monsters by their surrender to impulse, and they personify our latent fear that conceding to appetite will compromise our being and endanger other people.

Twilight illustrates this fear both in the danger that vampires represent to humans and in the concern that Edward and Jacob express regarding Bella's transformation. Less concerned with death than desire, Bella fears that her transformation will make her a "prisoner to her thirst."[49] Ironically, she is already captive to her own desire. She repeatedly falls victim to her all-too-human thirst for Edward, throwing herself at him at every turn. We both agonize over and delight in her abandon. At the same time, we are thrilled by Edward's self-control. Despite his powerful desire for Bella, he exercises restraint, stating that it is "mind over matter."[50] Edward, rather than being prey to his impulses, embodies our wish to subject our appetites to rational control.

Because the Cullens demonstrate self-restraint and strive not to kill humans, we can love them with less guilt; however, our guilt is not absolved altogether. *Twilight* not only illustrates the allure of vampires, it also articulates the ambivalence we have toward them. Meyer uses various means to achieve this end. As in classic works of vampire fiction, she uses gothic imagery, negative characterization, and graphic violence to cast suspicion on her shining subjects. From the onset, Forks is described in ominous terms. From the word itself, which alludes both to a flesh-piercing eating utensil and a point at which a precipitous choice must be made, Forks is presented negatively as an irrevocably gloomy place affected with "omnipresent shade."[51]

Similarly, while the vampires are described as beautiful, their beauty is inhuman. Though they possess a powerful physical appeal, they are also disturbing personifications of death. Their complexions are "sallow," "chalky pale," and they have dark "bruiselike" shadows under their eyes.[52] Their pallid skin is waxy and "frigid."[53] Their hearts do not beat, and they do not breathe. They are walking corpses. *Twilight* reminds us that vampires are as grim as they are glamorous by having them personify death and having them cause it. One of the most disturbing scenes in the saga occurs in *New Moon* where tourists are led like lambs to slaughter. Here, after our horror at vampires has nearly been dispelled by Meyer's romantic emphasis on Edward, it is resurrected. Meyer also questions the allure of vampires by having her vampires suffer self-loathing. Edward declares himself a "deplorable creature" and cries, "I don't want to be a monster."[54] Rosalie agrees, advising Bella to stay human. Bella too expresses doubt. She worries that she might turn into a monster, and this realization reinforces the notion that the life of the vampire isn't all that tasty.

Once Bitten, Twice Shy: Grave Concerns about Vegetarian Vampires

From an existential point of view, the questioning of the vampire mystique that occurs in *Twilight* is incredibly positive. Though anxieties central to the allure of vampires are completely understandable, the desire to forfeit humanity is not one that existentialists would endorse. As Alice Cullen recognizes in existentialist fashion, being human has its problems: "You don't get to be human again . . . [it is] a once-in-a-lifetime-shot."[55] Although existence confronts us with challenges and arouses powerful anxiety, it is nonetheless "a perfect free gift," a fullness that "man [should] never abandon."[56] Rather than work to undermine the appeal of vampires by foregrounding their inhumanity, *Twilight* asserts their superiority. In *Breaking Dawn*, Bella's initial concerns about being a vampire are dispelled. She awakes as a vampire "in wonder" to a "fairy tale" world with expanded senses and powers.[57] She can run all day and have sex all night. Instead of torturous thirst, Bella experiences "ecstasy in [her] new life."[58] She states, "I'd been so ready to string along my human time . . . I should have guessed . . . [being a vampire is] better."[59]

Being a vampire offers Bella complete wish fulfillment, particularly an escape from being weak and human and from the "years of mediocrity" that she assumes being human entails.[60] She achieves eternal life and love. She has a child and saves her species. She equals or supersedes in ability all of the vampires who used to personify her desires. She matches Edward's undying love and surpasses Carlisle's self-control, Esme's maternal devotion, Rosalie's beauty, Emmett's strength, Alice's loyalty, and Jasper's power over others. She doesn't feel the need to kill humans, so she isn't even a monster. Looking at Bella, it would seem that there isn't anything bad about trading in your humanity for fangs.

From the existential perspective, the delight Bella expresses at becoming a vampire is the problem with *Twilight*. It is a romance, not a horror story. With its captivating tale of star-crossed lovers, it seduces us into loving vampires more than we should. It casts Edward as the innocent and self-sacrificing Romeo, rather than as a compelling, but vicious monster. *Twilight* tips the scales in favor of vampires and fosters an unhealthy distaste for human life instead of showing a balance between the two.

So what is the problem with liking vampires? After all, they're not real. They don't really bite. If our engagement with vampire fiction not only entertains, but also helps us dispel anxiety, then it is all for the good. But does *Twilight* help us manage our anxiety, or reinforce it? While the anxieties we have about our condition are natural, Meyer's decision to celebrate Bella's forfeiture of humanity reinforces the notion that the human condition is flawed. Unlike other works that emphasize the desperate solitude and moral corruption of vampires, *Twilight* romanticizes them. Rather than foster the "ambivalent thrill" that contemporary philosopher Cynthia Freeland describes as having the potential to inspire a critical examination of our fascination with monsters, *Twilight* leaves no bitter taste.[61] Rather than encouraging us to appreciate what we have and make changes within our power, it encourages an escapist fantasy that degrades human existence.

The existential philosopher Friedrich Nietzsche (1844–1900) argued that the tendency to demean existence is born of "weariness with life" and an "instinct for revenge" on that which fatigues us.[62] Although life can make us weary, when this weariness is expressed as "hostil[ity]," it stands in dangerous "opposition to life."[63] Nietzsche argued that we need to affirm life rather than oppose it. *Twilight* is problematic because it demeans life and trades in impossible dreams that have the potential to cost us our lives. Not violently, of course. They bleed us slowly by directing our attention and appreciation from the life we have. Rather than alleviate anxiety, they aggravate it by encouraging our captivation with unachievable ideals.

Unlike Bella, we don't have the option of awaking to an eternal life or experiencing undying romance. As far as we know, we have only one life, and that life and our loves are painfully finite. For this reason, it might be wise for us to abandon our wish for eternal life and love, and realize that the aspects of the human condition that we sometimes suffer from are the things that make us what we are. We appreciate time by virtue of our lack of it, are sensitive because of our vulnerability, compassionate because of our dependence, and strong because of our fragility. While we can be monsters, we are more monstrous when we ignore our humanity than when we embrace it. Because they arouse and exacerbate our appetite for inhumanity, the humanistic vampires of *Twilight* are more deeply seductive, and ultimately more dangerous, than the vicious variety.

NOTES

1. Martin Heidegger, *Being and Time*, trans. by Joan Stambaugh (Albany: State University of New York Press, 1996), p. 177.

2. Ibid., p. 232.

3. Ibid., pp. 35, 235.

4. Jean-Paul Sartre, *Being and Nothingness*, trans. by Joan Stambaugh (New York: Washington Square Press, 1984), p. 796.

5. Stephenie Meyer, *Twilight* (New York: Little, Brown and Company, 2005), p. 476.

6. Stephenie Meyer, *Eclipse* (New York: Little, Brown and Company, 2007), pp. 109, 269.

7. Stephenie Meyer, *New Moon* (New York: Little, Brown and Company, 2006), pp. 10, 521.

8. *Eclipse*, p. 74.

9. Stephenie Meyer, *Breaking Dawn* (New York: Little, Brown and Company, 2008), p. 7.

10. *Eclipse*, p. 161.

11. *Twilight*, p. 339.

12. *Breaking Dawn*, p. 673.

13. Ibid., p. 741.

14. Heidegger, *Being and Nothingness*, pp. 409, 429.

15. Ibid., pp. 445, 463.

16. Albert Camus, "An Absurd Reasoning," in *The Myth of Sisyphus and Other Essays*, trans. by Justin O'Brien (New York: Vintage International, 1991), p. 13.

17. Joseph Epstein, "The Perpetual Adolescent," in *The Writer's Presence*, ed. by Donald McQuade and Robert Atwan (New York: Bedford, St. Martin's Press, 2009), p. 368.

18. *Eclipse*, pp. 119, 121.

19. *New Moon*, p. 6.

20. Ibid.

21. Ibid.

22. Ibid.

23. Ibid., p. 517.

24. *Breaking Dawn*, p. 27.

25. Ibid., p. 430.

26. *Twilight*, p. 46.

27. Ibid., p. 310, and *Breaking Dawn*, p. 190.

28. Ibid., p. 92, and *New Moon*, p. 539.

29. *Twilight*, p. 450.

30. *New Moon*, p. 29.

31. *Eclipse*, p. 109.

32. *Breaking Dawn*, p. 8.

33. Ibid., p. 293.

34. Ibid., p. 22.

35. *New Moon*, p. 382.

36. *Twilight*, p. 277.

37. *Breaking Dawn*, p. 422.

38. *Twilight*, p. 337.

39. *Breaking Dawn*, p. 466.

40. Ibid., pp. 398, 610.

41. Daniel Harris, "Celebrity Bodies," in *The Writer's Presence*, ed. by Donald McQuade and Robert Atwan (New York: Bedford, St. Martin's Press, 2009), p. 427.

42. Ibid., p. 367.

43. *Breaking Dawn*, p. 320.

44. Ibid., p. 430.

45. Ibid., pp. 393, 394.

46. Ibid., pp. 355, 477, 480.

47. Susan Sceats, "Oral Sex: Vampiric Transgression and the Writing of Angela Carter," in *Tulsa Studies of Women's Literature* 2, no. 1 (Spring 2001): 107.

48. Sartre, *Being and Nothingness*, p. 491.

49. *Eclipse*, p. 74.

50. *Twilight*, p. 300.

51. Ibid., p. 3.

52. Ibid., pp. 10, 19, 180.

53. Ibid., p. 137.

54. *Twilight*, pp. 187, 277.

55. *Eclipse*, p. 311.

56. Camus, *Nausea*, pp. 131, 133.

57. *Breaking Dawn*, pp. 386, 479.

58. Ibid., p. 527.

59. Ibid., p. 482.

60. Ibid., p. 523.

61. Cynthia Freeland, "Realist Horror," in *Aesthetics: The Big Questions*, ed. by Carolyn Korsmeyer (Oxford: Blackwell Publishing, 1998), p. 287.

62. Friedrich Nietzsche, *Twilight of the Idols: or How to Philosophize with a Hammer*, trans. by Duncan Large (New York: Oxford University Press, 1998), pp. 29, 68.

63. Ibid., pp. 49, 129.

BELLA'S VAMPIRE
SEMIOTICS

Dennis Knepp

Twilight is many things. It's a vampire story. It's a love story. But it's also a story of discovery. When Bella Swan learns that Edward Cullen is a vampire, she discovers a hidden world.

Like science fiction and fantasy authors, philosophers often write about hidden worlds. The philosophy of learning, discovering, and knowing is called *epistemology*. And *semiotics* is the part of epistemology that looks at the different kinds of clues used in discovering things hidden. Semiotics is ultimately the study of signs, because clues are signs that point beyond themselves and give us information. Bella, of course, learns to read the signs that point to *vampire*.

The Signs around Tyler's Blue Van

In *Twilight* chapter 3, "Phenomenon," Tyler Crowley's dark blue van slides on the ice in the parking lot and almost kills Bella. Somehow Edward saves her, even though he was "standing four cars down from me, staring at me in horror."[1] This is a mystery: How did Edward manage to save Bella? Bella finds several clues to this mystery. She notes that Edward is cold: "My head cracked against the icy blacktop, and I felt something solid and cold pinning me to the ground."[2] "I tried to get up, but Edward's cold hand pushed my shoulder down."[3] She sees the imprint of Edward's hand on the side of the van that was hurtling toward her: "Two long, white hands shot out protectively in front of me, and the van shuddered to a stop a foot from my face, the large hands fitting providentially into a deep dent in the side of the van's body."[4] "When they'd lifted me away from the car, I had seen the deep dent in the tan car's bumper—a very distinct dent that fit the contours of Edward's shoulders . . . as if he had braced himself against the car with enough force to damage the metal frame."[5] She hears Edward plead with her not to ask how he saved her: "The gold in his eyes blazed. 'Please, Bella.'"[6] She hears Tyler's confusion when she tells him that Edward saved her: "Cullen? I didn't see him . . . wow, it was all so fast, I guess. Is he okay?"[7] These clues lead Bella to believe that Edward is not quite like the other kids. Eventually she learns that the coldness, the hand imprint, the words are all signs that point to *vampire*.

The coldness, the deep dent in the van, and Edward's pleas are not random events. They are signs that point beyond themselves and give Bella information about a hidden world of vampires. Indeed, they follow an ordered pattern: one, two, and three.

These signs follow the triad of icon, index, and symbol. An *icon* is the simplest sign, the barest feeling: Edward is cold. An *index* is the result of physical interaction: the imprint of Edward's hand on the van. A *symbol* is a sign that gets meaning because someone makes the connection to that meaning: the words of Edward and Tyler.

1. Icon: simple feeling—coldness.
2. Index: interaction between two things—Edward's shoulder dents the van.
3. Symbol: words that get meaning from an interpreter—"Please, don't."

The Philosopher of Oneness, Twoness, Threeness

Perhaps the greatest theorist of semiotics is the American philosopher Charles Sanders Peirce (1839–1914).[8] Peirce (pronounced "purse") was a character who would have been more at home in Anne Rice's *Interview with the Vampire* than in Stephenie Meyer's *Twilight*.[9]

Isabella Swan and Charles Peirce are as different as two people could be. For example, Bella seems to have little or no interest in clothing or parties (she doesn't even want to go to the prom!). But Peirce dressed in "beautiful clothes" and traveled extensively in Europe even when he couldn't afford it.[10] Bella considers using cold medicine as a sedative to be a wanton misuse of drugs. By contrast, Peirce regularly used morphine, ether, opium, and cocaine (all legal at the time) to combat his various mental conditions, such as manic-depressive disorder.[11] Despite the supernatural events of her life, Bella has no problem conforming to the expectations of high school. But Peirce was regularly expelled, graduated near the bottom of his class, and could not keep a regular teaching job despite having family connections.[12] Throughout his life, Peirce had a difficult time conforming to conventional morality; and during the stuffy Victorian age, his reputation for "immorality" got him into trouble time and again.

Despite these differences, Peirce's theory of semiotics is useful for describing Bella's discovery. And thankfully a philosopher's theory should be judged by itself and not by the life of the philosopher. So even though Peirce's life wasn't particularly together, his semiotics might be. If it's a good theory of sign relations, it should apply to Bella's reading of the signs, too:

- An icon is a oneness. It's the simplest experience—the color, the smell, the taste of something. It is a feeling without any reflection. Peirce wrote that icons "serve to convey ideas of things they represent simply by imitating them."[13] It is the color of the sky, the smell of a rose.
- An index is a twoness—it involves the interaction between two things. A weather vane reveals the direction of the wind because the wind is pushing on it. A thermometer reveals the temperature because the temperature expands and contracts the mercury in the thermometer. Pointing at the moon is a connection between two things. Demonstrative pronouns ("this" and "that") are, too. A black eye is a sign of a fight because of the—well, you get the idea.
- A symbol is a threeness. This time the sign (1) points to the object (2) because someone (3) has made that connection. An octagonal-shaped piece of metal painted red with the white letters S-T-O-P is meaningless until someone reads it and stops her car. You have to connect that sign to the meaning "stop." A symbol must have a reader who connects the meaning to the sign. Words are the best examples, but there are others. If you see someone with pale skin wearing black clothing, bright red lipstick, and black fingernail polish, and her hair is combed over one eye, you would probably think, "Goth." Why? Because you know to connect those signs (black clothes, pale skin, red lips, etc.) to that meaning (Goth). That mode of dress does not by itself mean Goth—you have to make the connection.

The Sign of the Cross

Sometimes the same object can be all three sorts of signs. The best example in *Twilight* is the cross that Edward shows

Bella in the Cullen house. First, it is an icon—the distinctive color of the wood, "its dark patina contrasting with the lighter tone of the wall."[14] Second, it is an index—it points to the 1630s Anglican Church from whence it came. Third, it is a symbol—it is not just two pieces of wood. The cross is the symbol of Christianity. Peirce told us that "symbols grow," and this is a great example.[15] The Christian cross has multiple meanings and associations. Vampires are typically afraid of Christian crosses. So the fact that these vampires have a Christian cross displayed prominently in their home tells Bella that they're not your typical vampires. Furthermore, the fact that this particular cross is from Carlisle's father's Church gives Bella even more information about these vampires—they have a Christian heritage.

The Signs of a Good Vampire

Peirce went crazy with triads. He divided his original triad (icon, index, symbol) into further triads. For example, a symbol can be further subdivided into *word*, *sentence*, and *argument*. The best word for *Twilight* is "vampire." And the best sentence for *Twilight* is "Edward is a vampire." The best argument for *Twilight* is Bella's reasoning that Edward must be a good vampire because he tries to save her from harm.

But that's not enough. Peirce went even further with triads. He wrote that an argument can be further subdivided into three kinds: *hypothesis*, *deduction*, and *induction*.[16] A hypothesis is a guess—a possible explanation of strange events. Bella guesses that Edward is a vampire. More specifically, she guesses that Edward is a good vampire. This guess explains otherwise strange events. Bella's hypothetical argument follows this form:

- Edward acts like a vampire, but for some strange reason he won't attack me.

- If Edward were a good vampire, then it would not be strange that he won't attack me.
- Therefore, there is good reason to guess that Edward is a good vampire.

Notice that this argument doesn't inspire a whole lot of confidence. It's just a guess. Your logic teacher would probably dismiss this as a bad argument because the premises don't really support the conclusion. There could be other possible guesses: Maybe Edward just hasn't been hungry enough recently. But, that's okay. A hypothesis doesn't have to be 100 percent accurate. It's just a guess. It needs further evidence.

The second kind of argument, deduction, determines what that other evidence should be. You use a deduction to determine what follows from your hypothesis. We can think of Bella making the following deductions while on her trip to Port Angeles:

- If Edward is a good vampire, then he would save me from attackers.
- If Edward is a good vampire, then he will slow down his driving so I don't get scared.
- If Edward is a good vampire, then he will feed me when I'm hungry and let me sleep when I'm tired.

These if-then claims follow from Bella's guess that Edward is a good vampire. Now she knows what kind of evidence she'll need to either confirm or deny that hypothesis.

The last kind of argument, induction, confirms or denies the deductions from the hypothesis. Edward does save Bella from attackers in Port Angeles. Edward does take Bella to a restaurant when she is hungry. Edward does slow down his driving when Bella says that she's scared. Edward does let Bella sleep when she's tired. All of these confirm the hypothesis that Edward is a good vampire.

Vampire Semiotics Are No Guarantee . . .

Notice that this confirmation doesn't mean that the hypothesis is 100 percent accurate. There is always the possibility that other information can be found that will disprove the hypothesis. The evidence could have another explanation. It could all be a trick. Edward could just be toying with Bella, trying to get her guard down, so that he can eat her at another time. Bella could be wrong. Peirce calls this *fallibilism*: accepting the fact that even a well-confirmed hypothesis could turn out to be false.[17]

Bella learns this the hard way at the end of *Twilight*. While hiding in Phoenix with Edward's siblings, she receives a phone call from the evil stalking vampire, James. The thought process follows the familiar one, two, three pattern of Peirce's semiotics:

1. First is the icon: The voice sounds feminine.
2. Next is the index: It is the voice of her mother. Adding to that is the claim by the evil vampire that he has her mother. That brings Bella's thoughts to her mother much like a finger pointing at an object.
3. Then there are the symbols, the actual words said. Bella hears the words from her mother. She understands the threatening sentences from the evil vampire. And she formulates an argument about what to do.

Her argument about what to do is further subdivided into three categories. First is the hypothesis: (1) My mother is in trouble. (2) If I give myself up, then my mother won't be in trouble. So I must give myself up.

Next are the deductions. These are the if-then statements that follow from her hypothesis. If Bella is to save her mother, then she must go to the dance studio by herself. If she must go by herself, then she must evade Edward's siblings. If she can evade Edward's siblings and go to the dance studio by herself, then her mother will be saved. These deductions lead Bella into a course of action—now she knows what to do.

The inductions don't go so well, however. While trying to confirm the deductions from her hypothesis (I must give myself up to save my mother), Bella discovers that it is a trick. Her mother's voice was really just a recording. It was a trap! So the evidence disproves her hypothesis. It turns out that giving herself up won't save her mother. Semiotics gives no guarantee of truth. Signs can lead you astray.

The Semiotic Waltz: *One*, Two, Three, *One*, Two, Three, *One*, Two, Three

Once you get the hang of the semiotic waltz, it's easy to see the patterns of threeness in the world. Father, Son, Holy Ghost. Past, present, future. Mother, father, child. Location, velocity, acceleration. Human, vampire, werewolf.

But it's hard to see the point in all of this. Can't we just as easily divide the world up into fours? Or fives? The German philosopher Immanuel Kant (1724–1804) divided the world into twelve categories, and the ancient Greek philosopher Aristotle (384–322 BCE) had ten. So what makes three the magic number?

Peirce himself struggled with this issue and repeatedly tried to prove that three was the magic number. I confess that I'm not impressed by those arguments, and I won't restate them here. I suggest that we treat oneness, twoness, three-ness as a hypothesis—it is just a guess. We must figure out the deductions and try the inductions. That is, from this guess we should figure out what should follow and then test whether it does actually follow. And we should be fallibilists willing to reject this hypothesis if the tests come out that way. Peirce would never want us to accept his theory blindly—he would want us to test it.

So try it out. Test it. I provided three examples here from *Twilight*. (Why three? Isn't it obvious?) But there are three other books. Take a scene where Bella is discovering or learning and try to determine whether it fits the pattern of icon, index, and symbol.

NOTES

1. Stephenie Meyer, *Twilight* (Little, Brown and Company: New York and Boston, 2005), p. 56.

2. Ibid., p. 56.

3. Ibid., p. 58.

4. Ibid., p. 56.

5. Ibid., p. 59.

6. Ibid., p. 58.

7. Ibid., p. 60.

8. Since the 1980s, the Peirce Edition Project has been diligently working on a chronological edition with Indiana University Press that will serve as the standard for all Peirce scholars. But twenty years later, they have only published seven out of a proposed thirty volumes. That leaves out a great deal of good stuff from his later years. Fortunately, they published a smaller and easier-to-use two-volume collection. I'll be using the second volume: *The Essential Peirce: Selected Philosophical Writings:* Volume Two (1893–1913), edited by the Peirce Edition Project (Bloomington and Indianapolis: Indiana University Press, 1998), especially the 1894 essay "What Is a Sign?" on pp. 4–10.

9. The best biography of Peirce is Joseph Brent's *Charles Sanders Peirce: A Life* (Bloomington and Indianapolis: Indiana University Press, 1998). All the biographical material in this essay is from Brent's book.

10. "He always dressed, as long as he could possibly afford it, very well, with a rakish elegance. Henry James expressed his opinion of Peirce's personal style with a neat economy of phrase when he wrote his brother William from Paris, in 1875, that he had met 'Mr. Chas. Peirce, who wears beautiful clothes, &c.'" Brent, *Charles Sanders Peirce*, p. 25.

11. Ibid., p. 14.

12. Ibid., pp. 19–20.

13. Peirce Edition Project, p. 5.

14. *Twilight*, p. 330.

15. Peirce Edition Project, p. 10.

16. Ibid., pp. 287–288.

17. "Thus, the scientific Inquirer has to be always ready at a moment to abandon summarily all the theories to the study of which he has been devoting perhaps many years." Peirce Edition Project, p. 25.

sixteen

SPACE, TIME, AND VAMPIRE ONTOLOGY

Philip Puszczalowski

Who wouldn't want to be one of *Twilight*'s vampires? Imagine the things you could see and do if you didn't have to worry about death. Climb a mountain? Sure thing! Go over Niagara Falls without a barrel? No problem! Jump out of an airplane without a parachute? Piece of cake! Being a vampire is an adrenaline junkie's dream. You could cheat death at every opportunity and experience extraordinary things. But there's a slight problem with this scenario.

In *Twilight* we learn that vampires are "frozen" in the state that they died in. So how are they able to move at incredible speeds and lift cars off sweet-smelling teenage girls? Where do their supernatural abilities come from? After all, humans aren't capable of the amazing feats that vampires can perform.

Ontology is the branch of philosophy concerned with the nature of being or existence. When we ask what it means to be a vampire, we are asking an ontological question. We want to know what makes a vampire a vampire. How do we distinguish a vampire from a human? There are the obvious physical differences such as their pale skin, their exquisite beauty, and their need to drink blood for sustenance, but these things alone aren't enough to differentiate a vampire from a human. After all, doesn't everyone know someone like this? While these traits help to distinguish vampires from humans, we have to look deeper if we want to explain their supernatural strength and speed.

Kantian Space and Time

In the *Critique of Pure Reason*, Immanuel Kant (1724–1804) argued that knowledge can be divided into two different types: *a priori* and *a posteriori*. The latter is knowledge that is acquired through experience. The color of an object is a type of a posteriori knowledge. We know Edward's car is a silver Volvo because we've seen it. Edward's car could easily be blue, however. Color is an accidental property, which means the color of the car has no effect on the car. We can imagine it as any color we wish, but it's still Edward's car.

A priori knowledge is knowledge that we possess independent of an experience. If we separate all the unnecessary properties from Edward's car such as its color, shape, hardness, and so on, we are eventually left with one inseparable property: extension. This just means that no matter what the car looks like, how big it is, and so on, it must take up space. It's impossible to imagine a physical object without it occupying a certain amount of space. Extension, therefore, is a form of a priori knowledge for Kant. We know that objects must occupy space without having to encounter every possible object. This means we must have the notion of space *prior* to any perception of an object.

Like space, time is also a matter of a priori knowledge. Time, of course, is central to concepts like succession and motion. When Bella Swan drives her truck from Charlie's house to school, the distance she travels can be divided into successive parts. First she is at Charlie's house, then she is one block away, then two, and so on, until she arrives at school. This progression makes sense only if we understand it in terms of earlier and later (that is, in terms of time). Likewise, motion is the change of place over time. Obviously, one couldn't change locations if there were no time in which to do so. As with space, we can't imagine an absence of time. We can imagine a period of time without any objects, but we can't imagine an object without time (an object wouldn't exist if it didn't exist for any time). So, like space, time is something that we bring to the world in order to make sense of it.[1]

Kant revolutionized the way we think of space and time, arguing that space and time are not part of the world but instead are part of the mind. How we perceive the world is the result of how our brains are structured to understand it, and not how the world is actually structured. When Bella is still human, her perception of the world is limited. After she becomes a vampire, however, she perceives the world in a new way. Because of her heightened senses, she can see individual motes of dust floating in the air and hear car radios on the freeway miles away. The world itself hasn't changed. The dust and sounds exist while Bella is human and remain unchanged once she's a vampire, but Bella has changed. The physical limitations she experienced as a human have been removed.

Kant, Dracula, and *Twilight*'s Vampires

What was a year to an immortal?

—Bella, *New Moon*[2]

The vampires in the *Twilight* series differ from those in traditional vampire lore in many respects, but instead of examining every vampire legend, we'll use the vampire who became the template for modern vampire lore: Count Dracula. Dracula was based on the vampire legends of Europe, and since most vampires today are modeled after Dracula, he'll fit our purpose nicely.

Dracula shares much in common with the vampires in *Twilight*: being immortal, requiring blood for sustenance, and possessing tremendous physical strength.[3] Whether Dracula is stronger than Emmett Cullen is unknown, but I'd bet on Emmett in an arm wrestling competition. Dracula also has the power to hypnotize his victims, a power Edward Cullen appears to have as well.

There are, though, some notable differences between Dracula and *Twilight*'s vampires, such as Dracula's aversion to crucifixes and holy objects that have no effect on Edward and his kind. Where the vampires in the *Twilight* series really differ from modern vampire lore, however, is their ability to go outside during the day. While Dracula is merely weakened by sunlight, modern vampire lore heightens this weakness, making sunlight fatal to vampires.[4] Shortly after Edward rescues Bella in Port Angeles, we learn that most legends concerning the weaknesses of vampires are myth. It isn't until Edward takes Bella to his hidden meadow that we become privy to the sun's effect on vampires. Rather than bursting into flames, vampire skin sparkles in sunlight. This departure from modern vampire lore creates an interesting distinction between the ontology of Stephenie Meyer's vampires and the ontology of archetypal Dracula-vampires.

Although Dracula doesn't age, he is still affected by the passage of time. Dracula-vampires cannot come out during the day without being weakened or bursting into flames. The vampires of *Twilight* are not limited by the sun, and therefore, there is no temporal division for them between day and night. Their life is not endangered by being in sunlight. They avoid it because they want to keep their existence a secret.

Staying out of the sun is a self-imposed limitation (although one that's enforced by the Volturi). It isn't an ontological limitation. Thus, the vampires in *Twilight* are much more atemporal beings than Dracula-vampires. Could the absence of external time restraints explain their ageless quality? Perhaps, but given that we cannot think outside of space and time, we can only speculate.

Not only time but space is practically irrelevant for the vampires in *Twilight*. Supernatural speed enables vampires to traverse great distances very quickly. Because they don't need to breathe, they are excellent swimmers. And their incredible strength allows them to jump over (or move) any obstacle in their way. As a human, Bella is limited in terms of space; it takes her a long time to travel great distances by foot. Edward, by contrast, is able to travel short distances in the blink of an eye. Just think of the time when he rescued Bella from being crushed by Tyler Crowley's van. External space is compressed to the point of irrelevance.

Abilities beyond Space and Time: Alice, Edward, and Aro

Many of the vampires in *Twilight* possess special abilities. Alice Cullen, for example, can see the future. In addition to the fortunes of humans and vampires, she can predict trends in the stock market. (Sounds pretty good, doesn't it?) It's one thing to have supernatural speed and strength, but how are abilities like this possible?

Alice's ability to see the future is bound up with space and time. When Alice sees a possible future event, two things are occurring. First, she is seeing a future event in the present, which means she is experiencing the future as overlapping with the present. Time is being collapsed such that the time period between present and future is eliminated. Second, she is viewing one spatial event in a different, current space. When

Alice and Jasper Cullen take Bella to the motel to hide her from James, Alice "sees" James in the ballet studio while she's currently in the motel. Just as with time, she experiences one spatial event overlapping with another because the distance between these two spaces collapses. By suspending space and time, Alice blurs the boundary between present and future.

Edward's ability to read minds also manipulates space. Instead of being confined inside his own mind, Edward is able to hear the thoughts of others. His ability works over distance, allowing him to hear the thoughts of people in the same room, as well as the thoughts of people a few miles away. Essentially, Edward collapses the space between his mind and the minds of others.

Aro, one of the leaders of the Volturi, possesses a more powerful version of this ability. Aro is able to hear everything in a person's mind simply by touching the person. He hears not only what a person is currently thinking, but everything they have ever thought. While Alice can view a person's future, Aro is able to view their past. Aro collapses the past and the present, while Alice collapses the present and the future.

Since the past, present, and future are meaningless in the face of eternity, and space does not present an obstacle, we have a good clue here for understanding vampire ontology: they do not exist in space and time in the same way that we do.

When Worlds Collide

You are a magnet for trouble.

—Edward, *Twilight*[5]

One of the central themes of the *Twilight* series is the conflict between the worlds of Edward and Bella. Edward's world makes sense before he encounters Bella, and Bella's world, while drab, makes sense before she encounters Edward. It's only when Bella and Edward pursue a relationship that problems result for both. Edward exists in a world that is dangerous to humans, while Bella exists in a world that is largely ignorant of vampires. But perhaps the problems that Bella encounters because of the dangers vampires like James and Victoria pose are just manifestations of a deeper problem—namely, the conflict between Bella's imposition of Kantian space and time with Edward's suspension of it.

Consider how Bella is depicted as unathletic and clumsy, while Edward and his family are athletic and graceful. Alice always seems to be dancing when she moves, while Bella struggles not to trip over her own feet. Even their driving habits reflect this conflict. Bella drives her slow-moving truck, while the Cullens race fancy cars at dangerous speeds. Bella seems entirely limited by space, while the Cullens transcend space.

Bella is aware of this disparity, as she always remarks that time seems to slip by when she's with Edward, resulting in a muddled blur of both time and place. It's as if the speed of her world increases when she's with Edward and slows down when they part company. This feeling is rather common, especially when driving. Think of a time you didn't notice how fast you were actually driving until you got off the highway and slowed down. It's the same with Bella. When she's with Edward she doesn't notice time. But once she leaves his company, she returns to "normal" speed and it feels like everything has slowed to a crawl. While the high of new love certainly helps explain this experience, it may also be the result of Bella's limited world of space and time directly interacting with Edward's. The conflict between the worlds takes a dangerous turn, of course, at the major plot point in *Breaking Dawn*: Bella's pregnancy.

Previously, the struggle between Bella's and Edward's worlds never manifested in actual conflict. Yes, Bella was often in danger due to her encounters with the vampire world, but her world could stay separate from Edward's.

When Edward and his family leave the town of Forks at the beginning of *New Moon*, Bella is completely devastated, but she is not in danger. Her life goes on, as does Edward's. Once Bella becomes pregnant, however, the conflict between Edward's suspended Kantian world and Bella's world is no longer superficial. Her pregnancy creates a direct physical, biological, and ontological conflict between the world of humans and the world of vampires, threatening her life. If Bella has the child, she will likely die. Sadly, humans and vampires appear incompatible, at least at first.

The confluence of Edward's and Bella's worlds creates new possibilities that don't exist in Bella's world. When Bella becomes pregnant, she reaches full term in weeks instead of months. For humans, pregnancy is supposed to take nine months. Large, quick changes can be unhealthy for both mother and child. It's no surprise, then, that as Bella's pregnancy reaches the end of its term, Renesmee begins to damage her from the inside by breaking Bella's bones. Bella's world of Kantian space and time is in a life-or-death struggle with the suspended vampire world, and as we know, Bella's world loses. Only by turning Bella into a vampire, and removing the limitations of space and time, is Edward able to save her.

As we have seen, if the ontology of vampires involves the suspension of Kantian space and time, humans are at a significant disadvantage. And it turns out Bella was right to insist on becoming a vampire!

NOTES

1. For an in-depth explanation, see Immanuel Kant's *Critique of Pure Reason*, trans. by Norman Kemp Smith (New York: Palgrave Macmillan, 2003).

2. Stephenie Meyer, *New Moon* (New York: Little, Brown and Company, 2006), p. 57.

3. See Bram Stoker's *Dracula* (New York: Scholastic, 1971).

4. One need only look at recent television shows like *Buffy the Vampire Slayer*, *Angel*, and *True Blood*.

5. Stephenie Meyer, *Twilight* (New York: Little, Brown and Company, 2005), p. 174.

seventeen

FOR THE STRENGTH OF BELLA? MEYER, VAMPIRES, AND MORMONISM

Marc E. Shaw

Stephenie Meyer and I have a few things in common: We both went to Brigham Young University at the same time; we were both English majors there; and at some point, we both carried around a similar pocket-sized pamphlet. Like all active youth in the Church of Jesus Christ of Latter-day Saints (LDS or Mormon church), Meyer learned from a booklet given to every young man and woman: "For the Strength of Youth" which outlines the "shoulds" and "should nots" for those striving to live the faith.[1] The booklet gives counsel on a range of topics including dating, music, honesty, sexual purity, service to others, gratitude, education, tithes, Sabbath day observance, and friends.

What's Religion Got to Do with It?

But before getting too far into doctrinal details, perhaps you're wondering what Stephenie Meyer's personal religion has to do with the *Twilight* novels. After all, Bella Swan and most of the other characters in the saga are generally religion-free. Bella explains:

> Religion was the last thing I expected, all things considered. My life was fairly devoid of belief. Charlie considered himself a Lutheran, because that's what his parents had been, but Sundays he worshipped by the river with a fishing pole in hand. Renée tried out a church now and then, but, much like her brief affairs with tennis, pottery, yoga, and French classes, she moved on by the time I was aware of her newest fad.[2]

While the characters' actions in the series are not motivated by religious fervor, Meyer's "Unofficial Bio" on stepheniemeyer.com highlights her membership in the Church of Jesus Christ of Latter-day Saints. There she says that her religion "has a huge influence on who I am and my perspective on the world, and therefore what I write (though I have been asked more than once, 'What's a nice Mormon girl like you doing writing about vampires?')."[3] But it's actually not such a great leap from the teachings of the Mormon faith to vampires and the undead. Like Meyer's fictional world, Mormonism features a closeness between the realms of the living and the dead, the mortal and the immortal.

For LDS, the newly dead live temporarily in a spirit world that is another dimension of our very same world of the living. Indeed, living Mormons perform proxy baptisms for dead ancestors who never embraced the faith in their lifetimes. And, perhaps most pertinent to the *Twilight* series, the LDS believe in eternal marriage—that once you are married in the right place and by the right authority, your earthly marriage will be honored through life and death. That means love need never die (and in the eternities, the lovers need not die either). As a Mormon, Meyer believes that one day her body will be immortal and all-powerful, resurrected in a perfect form, together with her husband and sons forever. Sounds a little like Bella and Edward Cullen's transformation into immortal and powerful vampires, doesn't it?

Meyer's Religion and Its Philosophical Context

The *Twilight* series is a textual renewal of Meyer's faith and her commitment, which ties back to the teachings in the booklet "For the Strength of Youth" that she and I received as young people in the Church. One such renewal of that faith is the agency Meyer gives Bella. At the beginning of *Twilight*, Meyer places Bella in a new geographical location; she gets a fresh start where she stands at a new "fork" in Forks. Which path will Bella choose for her life, now that she is far from her mother and on the verge of womanhood herself?

In a sense, Meyer plays Heavenly Mother to her fictional daughter, Bella. In Mormon teachings, mortals leave the preexistent state—a world before this one where each spirit decides to come to Earth to be tested in the flesh. According to Mormon thought, God places us here in this life and leaves us with freedom to choose our path and be held accountable for our choices. This freedom and responsibility is known as *agency* in the Mormon faith, and it is one of the first ideas explained in "For Strength of Youth." Alas, there are, of course, consequences, sometimes eternal ones, for our earthly actions.

LDS thinkers did not originate the idea of agency, however. Rather, it is a central tenet of Christian philosophy going back at least to Saint Augustine (354–430 BCE), who called it "free will." While free will is a gift from God, unfortunately we all end up falling short in our use of the gift. Bella asserts her agency when she tells Edward in no uncertain terms that her choices and their consequences are her responsibility alone:

This has to stop now. You can't think about things that way. You can't let this . . . this *guilt* . . . rule your life. You can't take responsibility for the things that happen to me here. None of it is your fault, it's just part of how life *is* for me. So, if I trip in front of a bus or whatever it is next time, you have to realize that it's not your job to take the blame. You can't go running off to Italy because you feel bad that you didn't save me. Even if I had jumped off that cliff to die, that would have been my choice, and *not your fault*. I know it's your . . . your nature to shoulder the blame for everything, but you really can't let that make you go to such extremes![4]

We can't blame Edward for trying to save Bella, however. Throughout *Twilight*, Bella gives off the distinct feeling that she needs Edward-as-savior when her choices make her face danger: "I wanted nothing more than to be alone with my perpetual savior," she says in *Twilight*.[5] Like a Christ figure who pays for the sins of the one he loves, Edward cannot help but pick up some of the slack when his beloved falls short. Bella almost proves Saint Augustine's point that our own human actions are never quite good enough; sometimes, to be saved, we still need help from a higher power.

Meyer makes agency an issue for Edward, too. A "fork" in the road is there for Edward when he tries to fight his predestined state as a vampire:

[T]he majority of our kind who are quite content with our lot—they, too, wonder at how we live. But you see, just because we've been . . . dealt a certain hand . . . it doesn't mean that we can't choose to rise above—to conquer the boundaries of destiny that none of us wanted. To try to retain whatever essential humanity we can.[6]

Ironically, the more-than-human character wants his humanity to come through even more. He is determined to fight any sense of predestination.

Eternal Covenants, Binding Promises

Edward is no mere fallible mortal, and although he appears like a high-school homecoming king, he has walked the planet for much longer, making him mature and stable. Edward means business. He means what he says, and his words become actions. Just after Bella and Edward's first kiss, and their first (chaste) night together, the following exchange ensues:

> "I love you," I whispered.
> "You are my life now," he answered simply.
> There was nothing more to say for the moment.
> He rocked us back and forth as the room grew lighter.[7]

In this romantic moment with Bella, Edward's words *are* an action. When he says, "You are my life now," there is a union created in that utterance. Just like when a baseball umpire cries, "You're out!" and the base runner is out, or when a minister announces, "I now pronounce you husband and wife," the speaker's words literally perform an action. From the moment of that action, the future changes because of the speaker's utterance. Words can also be an action.

This idea comes from the philosopher J. L. Austin (1911–1960), who would call Edward's "You are my life now" a *performative utterance*. In *How to Do Things with Words*, Austin adds that when we know exactly what the utterance is performing (or what the words are doing), that "performative" is "explicit."[8] Do "explicit" "utterances" in Bella's bedroom sound like some sort of dirty talk? I am sure neither Austin nor Edward meant them as such. Instead, the words bind Edward and Bella together with a vow of consecration to each other. The words that Edward utters halfway through *Twilight* still hold meaning at the end of *Breaking Dawn*.

Eternal Union in Body and Spirit

As a Mormon who believes she is married to her husband for all eternity, Meyer relates to this never-ending promise. Mormons become "sealed" to their family members and believe that in the next life their immediate and extended family are joined. Bella and Edward obviously desire such a union. Although Edward thinks he is damned because of his vampire state, Bella cannot imagine herself in the hereafter without her companion: "Besides, the only kind of heaven *I* could appreciate would have to include Edward."[9] And Edward feels the same way, as Bella describes it: "He really did want me the way I wanted him—forever. It *was* only fear for my soul, for the human things he didn't want to take from me, that made him so desperate to leave me mortal."[10] We see this union in a different way in the joy that Bella constantly feels when Edward picks her up and carries her around with his strong body. She cannot help but be happy, even when other negative circumstances engulf them.

This union of the body and the spirit is nothing new in religion and philosophy. To get "erotic" for a moment, Plato's (428–348 BCE) dialogue *The Symposium* features a myth that explains the creation of love on Earth. In the beginning, there were three types of people who all had two heads with four arms and legs (eight total appendages). The three types of people were male/male, female/female, and male/female. At that time there was no need for love in the world because everyone was whole and happy. Feeling threatened by this wholeness, Zeus sent down thunderbolts that divided the people into what we would call humans today. Love was originated so that those who had been separated would be able to find their other half.

Plato's liberal view of love and sexuality clearly does not fit into the conservative LDS view of sexuality and potential marriage partnership. Mormon teachings allow marriage only between a woman and a man. Interestingly enough, though, in his *Time* profile of Meyer, Lev Grossman pointed out that the author's next novel, *The Host*—unrelated to the *Twilight* series—is

> set in the near future on an Earth that has been conquered by parasitic aliens who take over the bodies of humans, annihilating their hosts' personalities. One human host resists; she lives on as a voice in the head she shares with the alien. When host and parasite (who goes by Wanda) meet up with the host's old lover—now a resistance fighter in hiding—the alien falls for him too and joins the humans. It's a love triangle with two sides, a ménage à deux. Like *Twilight, The Host* is a kinky setup—two girls in one body!—played absolutely clean.[11]

Plato's *Symposium* seems to have made it into Meyer's writings after all. Or maybe the inspiration came from some old-fashioned, Mormon-fundamentalist *Big Love*.

Close but Not Too Close: The Erotics of Abstinence

Meyer walks a playful line between sex and no-sex in her *Twilight* series. The books are erotic, dangerous, and descriptive. Edward has to resist not only Bella's body but also her blood. Unlike other teenage heroes, Bella risks more than pregnancy: Her lover might destroy her completely. In his *Time* profile of Meyer, Grossman declares that the *Twilight* series is full of the "erotics of abstinence" because Bella and Edward get close but not *too* close—at least not until later in the series when the pair marry. The couple avoid the

premarital sexual "should nots" of Meyer's religion as out-
lined in "For the Strength of Youth." Because of the couple's premarital chastity, the LDS church-owned bookstores,
Deseret Book, gave Meyer's works prominent displays in
their shops throughout the United States. But more recently,
because of the erotic nature of Bella and Edward's abstinence,
some LDS members have asked the bookstore to remove
Meyer's series from the stores. Deseret Book struck a compromise by keeping the books available for special order.[12]

So, are the pair poster children for chastity? In the half-
page kisses Meyer describes breath by breath, the letter of the
law and the spirit of the law diverge. Grossman highlights a
scene "midway through *Twilight* in which, for the first time,
Edward leans in close and sniffs the aroma of Bella's exposed
neck. 'Just because I'm resisting the wine doesn't mean I can't
appreciate the bouquet,' he says. 'You have a very floral smell,
like lavender . . . or freesia.'"[13] Grossman argues that although
Edward "barely touches" Bella, "there's more sex in that one
paragraph than in all the snogging in *Harry Potter.*"[14]

But Laura M. Brotherson writes in the *Mormon Times*
(published by the Mormon-owned *Deseret News*) that Edward
is a "guardian and protector. It's like a lion falling in love with
a lamb. Thankfully for Bella, Edward comes from a family who has not only taught him to control his deadly appetite, but helps him do so as well."[15] Vampire family values!
Brotherson commends Edward's "sacrifice and self-discipline,
especially because it goes so against his natural wiring."[16]
Edward's ability to resist is "breathtakingly attractive" and
engenders confidence in Bella that she has found the right
(super)man: "It's little surprise to me that when Edward asks
Bella, 'Do you trust me?' there is no hesitation. How could
you not willingly give your whole life and anything else he
wanted, knowing full well he would never take or do anything
that would hurt you?"[17] But Bella does not fully *know*, really,
and that is part of the danger and eroticism Meyer creates.

Returning the Gaze

Meyer focuses on the carnal instead of the spiritual with her array of lengthy descriptions of Edward's looks. Because almost all of the *Twilight* series is told from Bella's point of view, and because Meyer fixates on Edward, *Twilight* returns the gaze that is usually reserved for men looking at women. Much feminist philosophy argues that men have customarily controlled the "lenses" of looking: whether photographic, filmic, theatrical, or even fictional (through descriptions in novels and other narrative forms). Customarily, the auteur/ author/director makes his audience gaze upon the woman's form with sexual desire. Meyer, however, makes us gaze through Bella's eyes at Edward's beauty. Edward is objectified, continuously sized up like a piece of meat at the market.

It's not simply a matter of making a sex object of the male (for a change). We are also aware of Edward returning the look: "Edward was staring at me [. . .] I stared back, surprised, expecting him to look quickly away. But instead he continued to gaze with probing intensity into my eyes."[18] Multiple times in *Twilight*, Bella stares at Edward, and he stares back. Instead of a unidirectional gaze that makes the other person a mere object of desire, *Twilight* offers a conversational, heartwarming, bidirectional gaze between the two young lovers.

Nice Mormon Girls and Sexy Vampires

We need to conclude by asking: Is *Twilight* properly Mormon? As with any text, there are multiple manners of reading and interpreting *Twilight*. And not all of Meyer's critics (professional and amateur; Mormon and non-Mormon) believe her *Twilight* series upholds the right standards. I hope this chapter has convinced you that it's at least possible for nice Mormon girls to write about sexy vampires.

NOTES

1. See "For the Strength of Youth," www.lds.org/youthresources/pdf/ForStreng Youth36550.pdf.

2. Stephenie Meyer, *New Moon* (New York: Little, Brown and Company, 2006), p. 36.

3. Stephenie Meyer, "Unofficial Bio," stepheniemeyer.com.

4. *New Moon*, p. 507.

5. Stephenie Meyer, *Twilight* (New York: Little, Brown and Company), 2005, p. 166.

6. *Twilight*, p. 307.

7. *Twilight*, p. 314.

8. J. L Austin, *How to Do Things with Words* (Oxford, UK: Clarendon Press, 1962).

9. *New Moon*, p. 37.

10. *New Moon*, p. 527–528.

11. Lev Grossman, "Stephenie Meyer: A New J.K. Rowling?" *Time*, April 24, 2008, pp. 34–35.

12. "Deseret Book pulls 'Twilight' series from shelves," www.ksl.com/?nid=148& sid=6243225.

13. Grossman, p. 34.

14. Ibid., p. 34.

15. Laura M. Brotherson, "Edward, Self-Mastery and the Marital Fire," MormonTimes .com, January 17, 2009.

16. Ibid.

17. Ibid.

18. *Twilight*, p. 73.

THE TAO OF JACOB

Rebecca Housel

The Tao is empty
When utilized, it is not filled up
So deep! It seems to be the source of all things

—Lao Tzu, Tao Te Ching[1]

Jacob Black has it rough. He's in love with a girl who's in love with a rich, handsome, smart, talented, immortal vampire. That's right, vampire. Who could compete with that? Well, thanks to the wisdom of the ancient masters, Jacob can. Although Jacob is fifteen when we first meet him, far from ancient and certainly no master, he shows a growing maturity common to young people who have experienced difficulties. Unlike typical fifteen-year-olds, Jacob cannot take life for granted. As a Quileute, he lives on the reservation, already aware of the social isolation connected with social difference; Jacob's father, Billy, is in a wheelchair and depends on Jacob for not just household chores but for increased mobility.

The *Tao Te Ching* describes a "way" or "path" (Tao) paved in the virtues of humility, compassion, and moderation. Jacob, having developed his emotional intelligence through difficulty, displays all three.

As the main text of Taoism, the *Tao Te Ching*, written by Lao Tzu over 2,500 years ago, focuses on the concept of Tao: "three jewels"—compassion, moderation, and humility— guide us on the Taoist path.[2] Even without taking on his shape-shifting ability as a wolf, Jacob, though younger (much younger) than Edward, has such wisdom. And while the Quileute creation legend of an ancient shape-shifter turning a wolf into the first Quileute man is true to the tribe's history, those aren't the ancients we're talking about here.[3]

Lao Tzu's reference to "ancient masters" in the *Tao Te Ching* may have been allusions to two "ancient masters" who were original influences in Taoism, Huang Ti (pronounced *Hwangdi*) and Fu Hsi (pronounced *Fu Shi*). Both Huang Ti and Fu Hsi were rulers of China approximately 4,700 years ago, or 2,200 years before Lao Tzu lived.[4] Huang Ti is associated with some of the earliest forms of Taoism, while Fu Hsi is credited with the yin-yang concept.[5]

It's Always Darkest before the Dawn

One of the most potent symbols of Taoism is the black and white circle known as yin-yang. Yin is passive, cold, dark, and soft. Yang is active, hot, light, and hard. Still, the two are not complete opposites—one flows into the other, and each has its place in the other, indicated by a dot of white in the black and dot of black in the white. In the world of *Twilight*, Jacob is yin. He knows Bella Swan is more interested in a relationship with Edward Cullen than with him. Although Jacob shows jealousy, it's never threatening. By constantly affirming that no matter what choices Bella makes, he will always be her friend, Jacob ultimately proves it. With compassion and humility as the foundation of his emotional intelligence, Jacob handles himself and others as a true Taoist.

Edward, by contrast, is yang. Lao Tzu said, "Wealth and position bring arrogance."[6] Edward acts aloof, "better" than others around him. He flaunts his wealth by driving expensive cars, wearing designer clothing, and looking down on humble possessions like Bella's truck. On the other hand, when Bella brings two discarded motorcycles to Jacob, enticing him to help her fix them by offering him one, Jacob is delighted. It does not matter to him that the motorcycles are not new or expensive. Because Jacob is grounded in humility and lives a life of moderation, he is more satisfied with life in general. Jacob understands that he isn't the center of the universe, and he's smart enough not to want that kind of power. As Lao Tzu said, "[H]e who knows that he has enough is rich."[7]

Edward does not have a yin bone in his arrogant body—and who can blame him? He was chosen by Carlisle Cullen to survive a fatal disease, and not just to survive, but to become stronger, faster, and smarter—for eternity. Typically, when people survive a fatal disease such as cancer, they emerge with a sense of humility, no longer taking for granted the mundane in life because there is no mundane any longer. Jacob's mother died when he was young, so he knows death and has an earned sense of humility from that experience. Additionally, he knows illness; his father is in a wheelchair. And because he knows death and illness, Jacob has developed compassion. He is also accustomed to moderation, living in a small house on the Quileute reservation and driving his father's beat-up vehicle.

Jacob is a true leader, not because he abuses his power, not because he is rich, and not because of extravagant promises. Jacob is a leader because he takes responsible action when necessary, regardless of his desires. He does not immediately claim leadership of the Quileute wolves, though it is his right; instead, Jacob yields that leadership to Sam until

Sam falters. Jacob thus illustrates the Taoist concept of *wei wu wei*, action by nonaction. The best type of action is often not aggressively forcing things, but allowing them to go their own direction. In the Taoist view, order and harmony are the natural way of things, and so we must get in touch with the Tao, with the natural interaction of yin and yang, to be in harmony with nature and the cosmos. To be clear, though, Taoism is not completely passive. It does not suggest that we should just accept whatever injustices come our way. There are times for action, but one must choose one's battles wisely.

At any time after Jacob learned of his ability to shape-shift into a wolf, he easily could have gone after Edward—but he didn't. Even when he knows that Bella is marrying Edward and her death will soon follow, despite his own feelings, Jacob attends her wedding—not an easy task. He warns Bella about Edward and cautions her about the decisions she is making, thus risking their friendship. Jacob does this because that is what good leaders do; good leaders do not necessarily do what is popular or what will make others happy. Even if it means jeopardizing a friendship or alienating a loved one, a good leader acts on his conscience.

When Edward comes to Jacob out of desperation, asking him to sire human children with Bella, Jacob does not jump at the opportunity. He recognizes it as his chance to be with the person he loves, even if imperfectly—but he is more than relieved when that is no longer an option. In fact, Jacob knows that his relationship with Bella is toxic to him, and so he separates himself from her several times throughout the saga in efforts to heal himself and let Bella live her life. By contrast, when Edward leaves Bella for "unselfish" reasons, Edward is cruel to Bella, hurting her deeply. It is Jacob who helps Bella learn to live again through a healthy friendship that encourages Bella to not only be herself, but also to become empowered by trying new things. Jacob does not ask Bella to change. He doesn't judge her clothing, truck, or choice of friends (except for Edward and the Cullens, and for good reason!). He's there for her, giving her respect and support—a true friend.

Edward, on the other hand, because he cannot have Bella (with *his* choice to cruelly reject her in efforts to "save" her), attempts suicide. Edward makes the choices he makes and continuously acts irresponsibly because humility is alien to him; arrogance is Edward's shadow. As Lao Tzu said, "Racing and hunting make one wild in the heart."[8] Edward literally races and hunts—he moves super-fast and must hunt regularly to sustain himself. Lao Tzu says that the ability to see, hear, and taste everything one desires makes that person blind, deaf, and unable to savor flavor.[9] This is the root of Edward's lack of humility, his weakness, and also the root of Jacob's strengths. Meyer seemed to want to create Edward and Jacob as the classic pair of Campbellian opposites, almost like two sides of the same coin, a yin and a yang.[10] While Jacob deserves the recognition of a good leader, because Jacob is humble, he will always withdraw himself, maintaining what Lao Tzu called the "Tao of Heaven." The Tao of Heaven is the light at the end of Jacob's dark tunnel.

No Good Deed Goes Unpunished

J. K. Rowling also creates yin and yang to drive her stories. Just think of Harry Potter and Draco Malfoy. The two contrast sharply, but are not complete opposites. As always, there is some yin in yang, and some yang in yin—a true balance. Malfoy is not necessarily a bad person, and Harry sometimes does bad things. Likewise, Edward may completely lack humility but he's not all bad. And Jacob, though lacking arrogance, makes his share of mistakes, too. The difference is that Edward is given undeserved consideration; similar to other beautiful "sparkly" people in society, like celebrities, he is forgiven for his transgressions, even rewarded for them.

Jacob represents the classic underdog (or underwolf, if you prefer): No matter how much good he does, how much he sacrifices, he is punished for it. The cliché, "no good deed goes unpunished," unfortunately applies to Jacob. But it's not really the fault of the characters. We can safely blame this one on the author. Rowling rewards her conscientious characters, whereas Meyer does not.

Jacob's life is compelling on many levels. He is isolated from larger society, living on the reservation. Because of his Quileute heritage, Jacob is burdened with the added responsibility of becoming a wolf—this is forced on Jacob and the others like him because of the existence of Edward and his family, who attract even more vampires to Forks. Jacob's mother is gone and his father is disabled, placing more responsibility on Jacob, including many household duties typically left to parents—even in being Billy's driver, Jacob assumes a more parental role. Yet Meyer chose to write another book, *Midnight Sun*, from Edward's perspective. Why? Edward gets everything he wants. Jacob doesn't. Yes, Jacob imprints with Renesmee in the final book of the *Twilight* saga, but to people paying attention, that's no prize. Should we blame Meyer for not giving Jacob his due?[11]

Luckily, Lao Tzu had the answer: "End sagacity; abandon knowledge; [T]he people benefit a hundred times."[12] This was Lao Tzu's way of telling people that not everything is about seeking knowledge in books; there is knowledge in life itself. Meyer rewards arrogance and punishes humility—that's a lot like real life. Part of Taoist philosophy is recognizing that knowledge comes from many different sources. It is not for us to scrutinize what is good knowledge and what isn't.

Bend So That You Don't Break

"Yield and remain whole; [B]end and remain straight," is Lao Tzu's advice on what to do in any conflict.[13] This may seem counterintuitive, but what Lao Tzu meant was that it takes more courage to yield, more strength to bend against your own desires, than to hold tightly to a position only to reach a breaking point. When an individual can do this in a conflict, the individual is rewarded with an open heart. Jacob is very unhappy about Bella's choices regarding Edward, though it is true that some of that unhappiness comes from Jacob's own desires to have Bella's love. But the greatest unhappiness for Jacob comes from the thought of a world without Bella as she is. Much of his pack has imprinted on their mates. And Jacob feels as though he is losing the only person on the planet he can be happy with when Bella chooses Edward, and in so doing, chooses death. Once Bella becomes a vampire, a "cold one" (a Cull-en), Jacob and she will be sworn enemies. The situation seems hopeless and helpless. But in the midst of this conflict, because Jacob truly loves Bella, and so truly wants her to be happy no matter what it means for him, he begins to yield and bend.

Jacob comes to see Bella when she and Edward return from their honeymoon, only to find her ailing from the accelerated pregnancy; it is literally killing her. Jacob expected Bella to be dead, or rather, undead—but at least part of her would still exist. The situation presented to Jacob when he first sees Bella's bulging belly is a completely new scenario: Bella is *really* going to die.

But the three jewels of Taoism come in handy for Jacob once again. His compassion for Bella's situation helps him to forgive her, his humility helps him to not judge her, and his moderation ultimately allows him to stay in and around the Cullen home to protect Bella and Renesmee from the Volturi, who are coming to accuse Bella and Edward of creating an immortal child, something forbidden in the vampire world. It is later revealed that Bella and Edward's situation is not as unique as everyone has imagined; a rogue vampire in South America impregnated human lovers as well.

The children of those unions are like Renesmee, vampire-human hybrids—not the aberrations the Volturi have out-lawed—where a human child is turned by a vampire's venom, forever frozen in child-form, and therefore, even more dangerous than adult vampires.

When Jacob first sees Renesmee, because he has the strength to yield and bend with his inner conflict about Bella, his heart is open and he is able to imprint. This was very convenient for Meyer, who undoubtedly wanted to give Jacob some kind of consolation prize for the character's incredible patience. While Renesmee has accelerated growth on her side, it will still be years before Jacob and she can ever be together romantically. In the meantime, Jacob gets to be her baby-sitter and primary source of blood at feeding time. As a shape-shifter, Jacob has increased healing, so the blood Renesmee will take from him does not hurt him as it would a typical human. Jacob's situation in *Breaking Dawn* goes way beyond compassion, moderation, and humility; but because Jacob is willing to bend, the reader knows he will not break.

The Dawning of a New Era

Of course Lao Tzu never imagined that a fictional character far in the distant future would exemplify the Tao. And Meyer herself probably did not realize how consistently she portrayed the character of Jacob within a Taoist framework. But whether you're on Team Edward or Team Jacob, you have to admit, Jacob is a pretty cool guy. If you're ever in a fight and need a buddy to watch your back, Jacob is your man (and not just because he has that whole wolf-thing going on either). Loyal to a fault, compassionate, and humble, Jacob is a true Taoist—even his deep connection with nature is consistent with Taoism. But what's most remarkable is how Jacob, almost broken by what is happening to Bella, manages to become whole again, despite his very real grief: "What the ancients called 'the one who yields and remains whole.' Were they speaking empty words? Sincerity becoming whole, and returning to oneself."[14]

Lao Tzu was speaking of Jacob here, even if he didn't know it. Jacob yields but still remains whole. The ancients Lao Tzu referred to, kindred of Jacob's old soul, were not speaking empty words. Ever humble, Jacob realizes that his opinions arc just that. Bella is not going to agree with him. Edward is not going to disappear. When Jacob stops feeling the need to be defensive, his heart opens. He sincerely becomes whole again, returning to himself. This gives Jacob leave to find his own happiness instead of wasting more energy on something he cannot change. If we could all be more like Jacob and follow the Tao, the world would be full of new possibilities.

As Stephen King said in his memoir, *On Writing* (2000), "I remember an immense feeling of *possibility* at the idea, as if I had been ushered into a vast building full of closed doors and had been given leave to open any I liked. There were more doors than one person could ever open in a lifetime."[15] Meyer's work has that feeling of possibility King describes so well—the books and films are only the beginning. Maybe Meyer will read this chapter and decide that Jacob's world is full of closed doors she can open to her readers. The *Twilight* universe has unlimited possibilities, and so does Meyer. A new dawn is breaking in the literary world.[16]

NOTES

1. Lao Tzu, *Tao Te Ching*, trans. by Derek Lin (Woodstock, VT: Skylight Paths, 2006), p. 4.

2. Some scholars theorize that the *Tao Te Ching*, while initiated by Lao Tzu, was added to by other anonymous authors throughout the centuries.

3. See "Quileute Tribe: Legends, Myths, and Folklore," www.quileutes.com/quileute-indian-reservation/quilayute-native-american-tribe-quileute-legends-and-quileute-monsters.html.

4. Lao Tzu, *Tao Te Ching*, pp. xv–xvi.

5. Yin-yang describes how seemingly opposing forces are interconnected and interdependent in the natural world, giving rise to one another. Jacob and Edward perfectly represent the idea of yin-yang.

6. Lao Tzu, *Tao Te Ching*, p. 9.

7. Ibid., p. 33.

8. Ibid., p. 12.

9. Ibid., p. 12.

10. In Joseph Campbell's *Hero Cycle or Journey*, Campbell refers to the necessity of a pair of opposites that the hero must transcend in order to have the necessary transformation of consciousness. See Joseph Campbell's *The Hero with a Thousand Faces* (Princeton, NJ: Princeton University Press, 1949).

11. "Rowling and Meyer, they're speaking directly to young people. The real difference is that Jo Rowling is a terrific writer, and Stephenie Meyer can't write worth a darn. She's not very good." This is a now infamous quote from author Stephen King. King has sold over 350 million copies of his more than sixty novels, short story collections, and other books. King celebrated the thirty-fifth anniversary of his first novel, *Carrie*, in April 2009. When Stephen King talks, the literary world listens. King calls himself the literary equivalent to a "Big Mac and fries"—acknowledging the commercial appeal of his accessible, yet engaging books. Meyer also writes accessible and engaging commercial books. Rowling, apparently richer than Oprah Winfrey, is clearly very good at her craft. However, it is not Meyer's responsibility to write well or not write well. It is the readers' responsibility to decide how to invest their time and money. While Meyer could not have foreseen the popularity of her books to gauge their potential influence, she must certainly recognize this now. And when it comes to fictional characters, the buck always stops with the author. See Brian Truitt, "It's Good to be King," *USA Weekend*, March 6, 2009, pp. 6–9.

12. Lao Tzu, *Tao Te Ching*, p. 19.

13. Ibid., p. 22.

14. Ibid., p. 22.

15. Stephen King, *On Writing: A Memoir of the Craft* (New York: Pocket Books, 2000), p. 15.

16. Thanks to Bill and Jeremy, but especially to Bob, who not only rocks my world but also challenges my ideas—a true Jacob. Love you!

CONTRIBUTORS

Ladies and Gentlemen, Introducing the Stars of Our Show, Humans, Vampires, and Shape-Shifters Alike

George A. Dunn, a lecturer at the University of Indianapolis and Ningbo Institute of Technology in Zhejiang Province, China, has contributed to several other books in the Wiley-Blackwell *Philosophy and Pop Culture Series*, including *Battlestar Galactica and Philosophy*, *X-Men and Philosophy*, and *Terminator and Philosophy*. His high school experience was remarkably similar to the Cullens': he kept to himself and tried not to bite anyone.

Eli Fosl is a student at DuPont Manual High School. When Eli's not thinking philosophical thoughts about vampires and shape-shifting wolves, he likes to hang out with friends, both living and undead. Let's just say Edward is very lucky Bella didn't meet Eli first.

Peter S. Fosl is professor of philosophy at Transylvania University. (Is that perfect, or what?) A specialist in the philosophical work of David Hume and skepticism, Fosl coauthored, with Julian Baggini, *The Philosopher's Toolkit* (2003) as well as *The Ethics Toolkit* (2007). Aside from his work as a teacher and scholar at Transylvania, Fosl has been conducting nocturnal experiments on the effects of bourbon upon human blood, which seems to make him immune to vampire venom. For those specially chosen, he leads tours of the university crypt (for real).

Rebecca Housel was a professor of writing, popular culture, film, and philosophy deep in remote western New York as a "normal" human for fifteen years. She is now a freelance writer and editor, where she can work from home in her true form. Rebecca edited *X-Men and Philosophy* (with J. Jeremy Wisnewski, 2009) and has written articles on poker, superheroes, Iron Man, and Monty Python for the series. When she's not writing, Rebecca prowls the mountainous regions of New York for the "cold ones." A true vegetarian, she hopes never to find any.

Jean Kazez teaches philosophy at Southern Methodist University. She is author of *The Weight of Things: Philosophy and the Good life* (2007) and *Animalkind: What We Owe to Animals* (forthcoming). She writes a regular column on the arts in *The Philosopher's Magazine* and has written about ethics, religion, happiness, and parenthood for several magazines. Jean also enjoys spending time with her vampire relatives, though none have ever met Bella or Edward.

Dennis Knepp teaches philosophy at Big Bend Community College. His essay "Bilbo Baggins: The Cosmopolitan Hobbit" will appear in the forthcoming *The Hobbit and Philosophy* (2010). He suggests Bella and Edward move to eastern Washington's Columbia Basin, where the frequent sunny days would make them sparkle like diamonds.

Bonnie Mann is an assistant professor of philosophy at the University of Oregon. She tries to get to Washington State as often as possible to have tea with Alice and Bella. Sometimes she gets to baby-sit Renesmee, but only if Jacob is there to feed her. Because of her relationship with the Cullens, Bonnie can honestly say that their home is just like it looks in the movies.

Leah McClimans was a philosopher by day, vampire hunter by night until her husband foisted *Twilight* on her in the hopes of reclaiming some of those evening hours. Now, when the philosophy is finished, she spends her free time campaigning for vegetarian rights and arguing with her husband over whether she can become a vampire.

Jennifer L. McMahon is an associate professor of philosophy and chair of the Department of English and Languages at East Central University. McMahon has expertise in existentialism, aesthetics, and comparative philosophy. She has published extensively in the area of philosophy and popular culture. Her most recent publications include essays in *The Philosophy of TV Noir* (2007), *The Philosophy of Science Fiction Film* (2007), and *House and Philosophy* (2008). While she sees why people are attracted to vampires, she's really a dog person.

Nicolas Michaud is a roaming philosopher. He stalks the Art Institute of Jacksonville, Florida; Community College Jacksonville; Jacksonville University; and the University of North Florida in order to feast upon innocent students and change them into philosophers. He was inspired to write about *Twilight* by the love of his life: Jessica Watkins. If it weren't for her, he never even would have read the books. He'd call her his "Bella," but Jessica is far more wonderful.

Abigail E. Myers is a freelance writer and teacher in the New York City public schools. She coauthored "U2, Feminism, and the Ethics of Care" with Jennifer McClinton-Temple for *U2 and Philosophy*. Her *Twilight* books would disappear for months at a time, "borrowed" by her eighth grade students. Every time Abigail opens her closet, she wishes Alice were there to give her some ideas.

Philip Puszczalowski is a Ph.D. candidate in philosophy at the University of Calgary. His research interests include existentialism, Nietzsche, and ethics. Despite what his sister thinks, a vampire would easily beat a werewolf in a fight.

Marc E. Shaw is an assistant professor of theater arts at Hartwick College. His recent publications include two chapters in anthologies: one about Harold Pinter's *The Dumb Waiter* and another about the images of masculinity in Neil LaBute's plays. Although Marc is not a vampire, his pasty whiteness is as translucent and frightening as Edward's—and almost as sexy. Almost.

Brendan Shea is a Ph.D. candidate in philosophy at the University of Illinois, where he works on issues in the philosophy of science. He teaches courses in ethics, logic, and the history of philosophy. While grading papers recently, it occurred to him that a policy of regular mind reading would be a more efficient means of measuring student knowledge. He plans to implement this new procedure as soon as possible.

Eric Silverman is assistant professor of philosophy and religious studies at Christopher Newport University. His interests include medieval philosophy, ethics, and philosophy of religion. His first book, expected to come out next year, is titled *The Prudence of Love* and argues that possessing the virtue of love advances the lover's well-being. However, he is convinced that hanging out with werewolves and vampires tends to undermine one's well-being.

Andrew Terjesen is a visiting assistant professor of philosophy at Rhodes College. He previously has taught at Washington and Lee University, Austin College, and Duke University. Andrew is very interested in the philosophical aspects of empathy and related topics, writing on those issues in contributions to *The Office and Philosophy* and *Heroes and Philosophy*. Were he to become a vampire, his "gift" would undoubtedly be some form of super nonchalance.

Jenny Terjesen lives in Memphis, Tennessee. When she's not reading the *Twilight* series, Jenny is a bloodsucking HR manager.

J. Jeremy Wisnewski, being a vegan, never craves blood but is drawn to vampires all the same. He coedited *Family Guy and Philosophy*, *The Office and Philosophy*, and *X-Men and Philosophy* (with Rebecca Housel). And there are more in the works (*Arrested Development and Philosophy*, anyone?). Although he felt guilty about being so taken in by *Twilight* at first (because he's a snob), he quickly got over it. Vampires rule!

Sara Worley is associate professor of philosophy at Bowling Green State University. She has published primarily in philosophy of mind, although her interests in recent years have turned more toward philosophy of psychiatry. Despite years of trying, Sara has not yet managed to develop a taste for mountain lions. Grizzly bears, however, are another matter.

Naomi Zack is professor of philosophy at the University of Oregon. Her recent books include *Inclusive Feminism* (2005) and *Ethics for Disaster* (2009). While living in the Pacific Northwest, Zack has met several people who have had dinner with Bella and Edward.

INDEX

For Those Who Can't
Read Minds